Cover: *Lenin at the VII All-Russian Meeting of the Soviets, in Moscow, March 1918*
pastel sketch on paper, 13 × 16·5 cm.

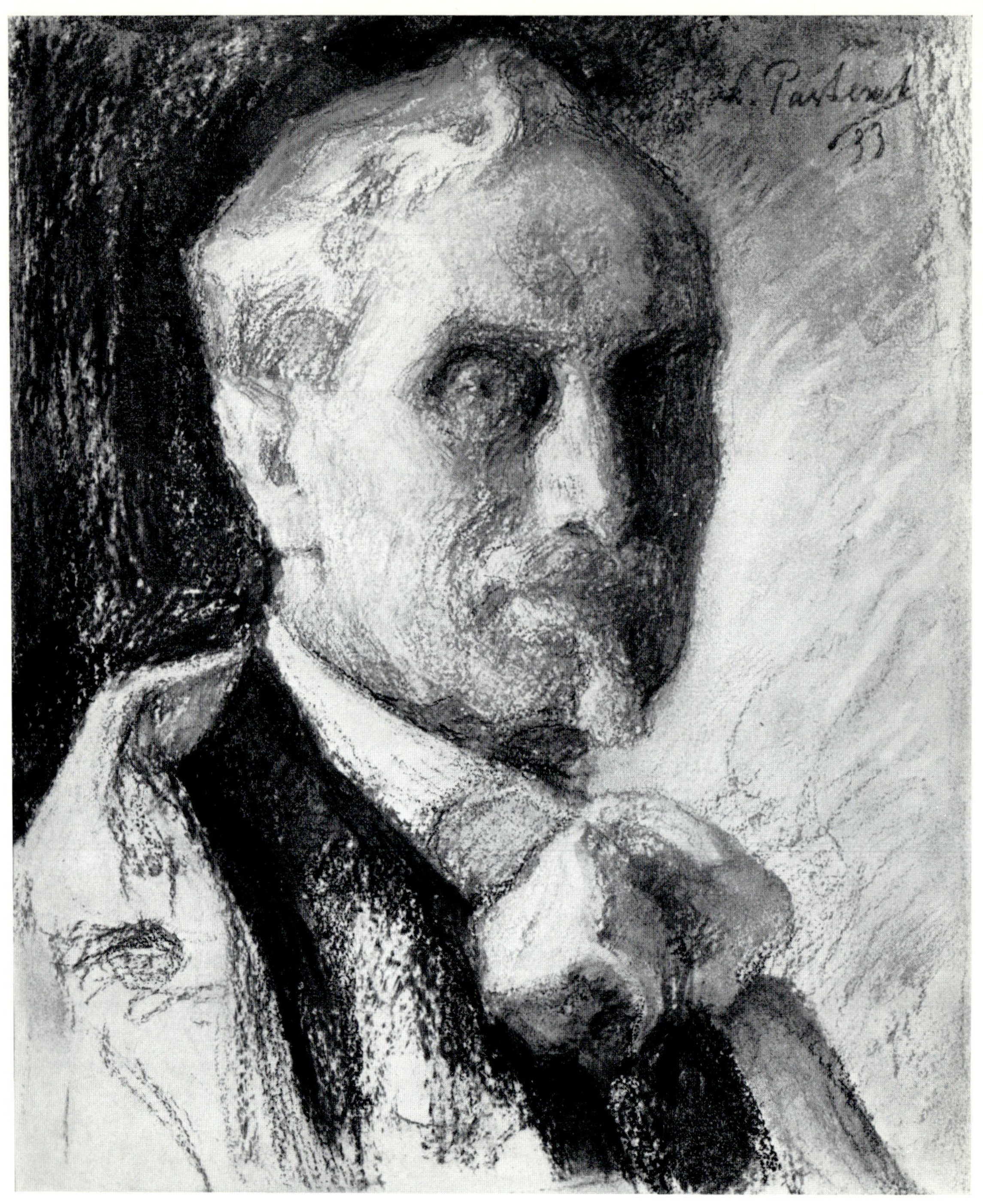

Self Portrait, 1933, pastel on paper, 41 × 32·5 cm.

Leonid Pasternak

A Russian Impressionist

1862–1945

by David Buckman

Published by the

Maltzahn Gallery Ltd

3 Cork Street, London W1

© 1974 David Buckman

Published by the Maltzahn Gallery Ltd

Distributed to the trade by
Lund Humphries Publishers Limited
12 Bedford Square, London WC1

SBN 85331 379 2

Designed by Graham Johnson/Lund Humphries
Printed in Great Britain by Lund Humphries, London and Bradford

Introduction

Early in 1957 a letter appeared in the correspondence columns of *The Times* from the former president of the Royal Academy of Arts, Sir Alfred Munnings, on 'Exchanging Views with Russians'. He recalled wartime co-operation with the Moscow Art Society which had led to an exhibition of works by Soviet war artists at the Academy and now pleaded for a big London show of the Russian school there. He was sure it could be as huge a success as other Academy exhibitions of foreign schools had been.

'I am not speaking in ignorance,' he continued, 'for in my twenties, when full of energy, I often went abroad visiting galleries at The Hague, Amsterdam, Berlin, Dusseldorf, Leipzig, Dresden, and Munich – spending days in great collections of old masters and new. But it was in the modern galleries of that day that I revelled in the works of European painters of the period and believe me or not, some of the best were by Russian artists: figure subjects, landscapes, and interiors; one that I loved – a lamplight scene of the Tolstoy family at home.'[1]

Out of thousands of canvases seen and over several decades Sir Alfred had remembered especially that Tolstoy picture – *Tolstoy with his Family*. The surname of the painter is internationally famous, Pasternak – not Boris, poet and author of *Dr. Zhivago*, but Leonid, his father. Dozens of museums and galleries in his native Russia and many public and private collections throughout the world contain his works, but events during his lifetime inhibited the establishment of a popular reputation. The only book about him is now a collector's item, in German, published many years ago.

Pasternak spent his last years in Oxford. Since his death, in 1945, efforts by his daughters, who still live there, have brought about a number of exhibitions of Pasternak's works, which have proved a revelation to those lucky to have seen them. The object of this monograph is to provide background information on Pasternak, and for the Western reader to sketch in the Russian artistic scene in which he grew up, so that his place in it may be better understood. Recognition is long overdue to Leonid Pasternak – illustrator of Tolstoy, portrayer of famous men, influential teacher, founder-member of the Union of Russian Artists and fine Impressionist painter.

DAVID BUCKMAN

Acknowledgements

The preparation of this monograph would have been impossible without the tireless assistance of Leonid Pasternak's elder daughter, Josephine, who has given many hours to talking about her father, translating material and assisting with its selection. She and her sister, Lydia Pasternak-Slater, also made many useful suggestions about the typescript and helped correct the proofs. Charlotte Haenlein gave invaluable help with translating and research.

I am grateful to the editor of *Burke's Peerage & Burke's Landed Gentry*, Commander Douglas C. V. Pelly, and Mary White, of the E.E.T. & P.U., for information about Esher Place and Lord D'Abernon. Other facts came from the British Library, Westminster Central Reference Library and Fine Arts Library, Marylebone Road Library, St. Pancras Library, Tate Gallery, British Museum, Kunstbibliothek, Berlin, and the Belgian and French Embassies, in London.

Permission has been granted to use certain copyright material, cited in the list of references. Thanks are due to the trustees of the estate of Sir Alfred Munnings, George Allen & Unwin Ltd., William Collins Sons & Co. Ltd., Paul Elek Ltd., Thames & Hudson Ltd., Chatto & Windus Ltd., W. W. Norton & Co. Inc., New York, the Ashmolean Museum, Oxford, and the editor of the German magazine *Westermanns Monatshefte*.

I am also grateful to the Musée National d'Art Moderne, Paris, for supplying the print of *Students Before the Examinations*, to the Tretyakov Museum, Moscow, for *A Letter from Home*, to the Russian State Museum, Leningrad, for *Tolstoy with his Family* and *Staff Meeting at the Moscow School of Painting, Sculpture and Architecture*, and to all these museums for permission to reproduce the photographs here.

Imre von Maltzahn, who commissioned this book on behalf of the Maltzahn Gallery, would like to acknowledge his gratitude here to Ian Robertson, formerly of the Ashmolean Museum. It was his enthusiasm for Leonid Pasternak's work and introduction to the artist's daughters that led to the 1974 exhibition at the Maltzahn Gallery.

© David Buckman, 1974

Chronology

1862 Born 4 April, in Odessa
As small boy develops an interest in drawing, despite parental opposition

1875 Completes self-portrait, when aged 13

1879 In final school year is allowed lessons at the Odessa School of Drawing. Contributes to magazines

1881 Studies medicine at Moscow University, but is unable to gain part-time place at Moscow School of Painting

1882 Again unable to study at Moscow School, so works privately under Professor E. Sorokin

1883 Having abandoned medicine, begins studying law at Odessa University. Enables him from October to spend several terms at Munich Academy

1885 Having graduated in law, completes a year's military service in Odessa
Meets Rosa Kauffmann, the pianist

1888 In Moscow paints large *genre* canvas *A Letter from Home*, bought by Pavel Tretyakov for his gallery. It is exhibited at the Wanderers' show

1889 Marries Rosa Kauffmann. They move to Moscow permanently
Visits Paris, where he sees work of French Impressionists
Gets to know Vassily Polenov and Moscow *avant-garde* artists
Works on periodical *The Artist* and Konchalovsky's jubilee Lermontov edition as art director
Establishes own school

1890 Son Boris is born

1892 *The North* magazine asks him to illustrate Tolstoy's *War and Peace*

1893 Start of friendship with Tolstoy. Second son, Alexander, is born

1894 Appointed to staff of the Moscow School of Painting

1898 Invited by Tolstoy to illustrate *Resurrection*
Exhibits with World of Art group in St. Petersburg

1900 Visits Paris, where canvas *Students Before the Examinations* is acquired for Luxembourg; it and *Resurrection* drawings are exhibited at Paris Universal Exhibition. Daughter Josephine is born
Helps to found group 36 Artists in Moscow, forerunner of Union of Russian Artists

1902 Second daughter, Lydia, is born

1903 Exhibits at first Union of Russian Artists show, in Moscow

1904 Visits Italy

1905 Elected Member of the Academy of Fine Arts. Revolution closes the Moscow School, so Pasternak spends several months in Berlin, where he gets to know Corinth, Liebermann and other German artists

1907 Travels in Holland, Belgium and England

1910 Paints Tolstoy on his deathbed

1912 Visits Germany and Italy

1914 Lithograph *The Wounded Soldier* is a great popular success

1921 Moves to Berlin

1923 Monograph on Rembrandt published

1924 Travels in Egypt and Palestine

1927 First one-man exhibition at Galerie Hartberg, Berlin

1932 Second one-man exhibition at Galerie Hartberg. Max Osborn's monograph on Pasternak published

1938 Visits London and prepares for return to Moscow

1939 Death of Rosa Pasternak. Moves to Oxford. Start of long period of illness

1945 Dies in Oxford on 31 May, aged 83

Location of Works

It has not been possible yet to compile a comprehensive catalogue of Leonid Pasternak's work. Much has remained in Russia. Examples are to be found in the Tretyakov Gallery, the Tolstoy and Gorky Museums and the Lenin State Library, in Moscow, in the State Russian Museum and Tolstoy collections, in Leningrad, in the galleries of Smolensk, Odessa and many other cities, as well as in private hands.

Outside the Soviet Union Pasternak's pictures are known to be in most European countries, in the Americas, in Asia and in Australia. Apart from private collections in the West, notable examples are in the Berlin Kupferstichkabinett; Musée National d'Art Moderne, Paris; in Britain in the British Museum, Tate Gallery and Victoria and Albert Museum, London, the Ashmolean Museum, Oxford, and in the city art galleries of Bristol, Birmingham and Southampton; at Harvard, in America; in the University of Jerusalem and various galleries in Israel.

Leonid Pasternak

Early Life

Leonid Osipovich Pasternak was born in Odessa on 4 April 1862 into a large, poor family. He was the youngest of nine brothers and sisters, three of whom died in infancy, another as a schoolboy. Pasternak's father had taken the lease of a big yard to which was attached a small, eight-room guesthouse, which offered hospitality to farmers and cattle-drovers.

The life of Odessa, a southern port populated by lively people of mixed Russian and Latin blood, left an indelible impression on Pasternak. The unusual variety of visitors who daily poured into his father's huge yard constantly excited the children's interest – groups of Ukrainian peasants who arrived with their corn in rattling carts, majestic oxen, the ancient carriages of modest landowners, the last representatives of a dying feudal class, and Tartar hawkers in their colourful national costumes. It was a whole universe, where he spent most of the day – playing, dreaming and observing, Pasternak recalled, when writing his memoirs in old age.[2]

Leonid started to draw very early, keen to record these picturesque impressions. His first patron was a yard-keeper, who commissioned hunting scenes with greyhounds chasing hares. 'It now seems incredible to me,' writes Pasternak, 'that as a boy of six to seven I was capable of fulfilling my customer's orders to his full satisfaction. For each hunt I got 5 copecks which I spent immediately to buy sweets for myself and my sister Assia.'

From the beginning of their marriage Leonid's parents had suffered economic hardship. His mother carefully saved every penny to send the youngest children to grammar school to give them the chance of a civilised adult life. School provided further scope for Pasternak's artistic abilities although he had no special art lessons there. However, his talent was noticed by the headmaster, who asked him to attempt such subjects as a portrait of the school's trustee or a picture to celebrate an imperial occasion. A self-portrait completed by Pasternak at the age of only 13 years reveals considerable natural ability.

It is probable that the headmaster had seen a clandestine humorous journal which Pasternak produced for circulation among his schoolfriends. This contained caricatures of the masters and commented on topical events. Because of the strict school regime Pasternak had to keep this activity secret, and it was not until he had left school that he learned his publication had had an eager and amused regular readership in the staff common room. In the senior form at school Pasternak was competent enough to earn a little money by contributing a number of comic drawings to professionally produced magazines.

These developments received no encouragement at home, where Pasternak's father imposed a spartan regime. He was determined that the application of puritan principles would produce children who were morally upright, industrious and self-reliant. Strict discipline, even the eradication of natural tenderness between parents and children, was the rule. When they learned that Leonid wanted to be a professional artist the Pasternaks were dumbstruck. They knew nothing about art, but they were sure that a professional painter must face years of poorly paid insecurity, the very circumstances that they had worked to escape. They tried persuasion and threats – his mother in her desperation even burnt Leonid's drawings. However, when he was in his final year at school – 1879–80 – the boy was reluctantly permitted by his father to attend the Odessa School of Drawing for some lessons.

In later years Pasternak was to look back on his parents' efforts to thwart his artistic aims without rancour. His mother, a frail, humble woman, he remembered as 'an angel of kindness', and to her he attributed his love of nature, flowers and colours. To his father Leonid was sure he owed the gift of observation and the psychological insight which was to become a noted feature of his mature portraits. For the severe and proud man who had normally abhorred frivolity could on occasion be persuaded to entertain his children with parodies and impersonations which revealed great natural talent and psychological perception.

'My father knew from his earliest childhood what he was going to be,' Leonid Pasternak's younger daughter, Lydia, recalls.[3] 'In spite of all the discouragement he received at home, he never had the slightest doubt about his calling as an artist, and never regretted following it. I am emphasising this point, as it has been suggested that he really longed to become a doctor, and that Yuri Zhivago was partly modelled on him – a rather absurd suggestion. True, while pursuing his art studies, first in Moscow, then in the Munich Academy, he also entered the university as a medical student, soon changing over to, and graduating in, law; but this was done solely for the sake of his parents.' His 'unquestionable loyalty and integrity, with an exaggerated sense of responsibility and duty' led him to adopt this course.

Thus in 1881 Leonid agreed to enter Moscow University to study medicine, his mother having long-standing ambitions for him to become either a doctor or a lawyer. Leonid chose Moscow because he hoped to enrol simultaneously at the famous Moscow School of Painting, Sculpture and Architecture. It was the dissecting room that eventually turned Pasternak away from medicine towards law. 'However, I mastered the science of anatomy,' he writes, 'so useful to a painter for his knowledge of the forms of the human body.'

In fact he gained excellent marks in these examinations, although he was less successful in his attempts to continue his art studies. The year that he arrived in Moscow he was unable to take a course there, as the School of Painting's term had already begun. The following year he was again unlucky. There was just one place left when he applied, which went to a young woman. Not to waste time, Pasternak decided to combine his university studies with several months' artistic tuition in the studio of an academician, Professor E. Sorokin.

Some years later, when he was a professor at the Moscow School, Leonid thumbed through the class register for that second year when he had been an unsuccessful applicant there. He discovered to his amusement that the young woman who had deprived him of a place was Tatyana Lvovna, daughter of Count Leo Tolstoy, both of whom were by then his friends. 'We laughed about that curious incident,' he writes, 'and T.L. said that I owe it to her that, not having been able to enter the School, I decided to go abroad and become a student of the Munich Royal Academy of Art.'

His Moscow School disappointments had not blunted Pasternak's determination to obtain a thorough art training. Because of Odessa University's relatively easy-going attitude he decided to leave Moscow and enrol there. That done, he found it possible whilst studying law at Odessa to get permission to travel to Munich, where for several terms commencing October 1883 he attended the Academy. The money Leonid had saved from his magazine illustrating paid his fares to Munich and home again during the vacations.

With such teachers as Ludwig Herterich, Franz von Defregger and Alexander von Liezen-Mayer in attendance, the Munich Academy had a wide reputation as a centre of sound draughtsmanship. Pasternak had no reason to fear for his progress. Having topped the list at the entrance examinations, he remained in this position in his class during his time at the Academy. Herterich apparently was often so satisfied with his pupil's work that he left it uncorrected. Several years later these drawings were to become sought after among connoisseurs in Moscow and were to help establish Pasternak's name there.

The money he had saved and the subsistence allowance made available by his parents were so meagre that Leonid's Munich life was tough. He writes affectionately of 'Good old Munich', of the tuition he received, its inhabitants, its customs and the treasures in its museums. Yet often he would have to walk round these museums with an empty stomach, as 'there was not money enough for such a frugal dinner as horseradish with bread'. However, he was able to repay his parents by not only being a star pupil at Munich but also by graduating in law from Odessa University, to them far more important.

The price he paid was a deterioration in health, which necessitated a return to Odessa to recover. He was, anyway, a little disenchanted with the painting classes at the Academy, which were less exciting than the drawing classes there. He was taken with the new achievements and lighter palette of contemporary French painters, and decided that after sorting out certain matters in Odessa – completing his military service and final legal examinations – he 'would be free to go and live in Paris, then the source of living art'.

In Odessa, however, he met Rosa Kauffmann. This event was to deflect him from his immediate plans. Meeting Rosa presented him with one of the two big decisions of his life.

Rosa Kauffmann and Marriage

In his memoirs Leonid Pasternak tells how Rosa Kauffmann opened the world of music to him. Not only was it to bring him pleasure but also to affect his own work. The blending of the two artistic spheres is to be found in some of his finest mature canvases and drawings: the series of portraits of composers and musicians, Rachmaninov, Scriabin, Chaliapin, Rubinstein, Heifetz, Eisner, Elman, Prokofiev, and many others. Then there are compositions such as Kussevitzky conducting with Scriabin at the piano, Nikisch conducting in the former Nobility Assembly, the Rachmaninov Trio, and historical works such as Bach and Frederick the Great.

When Pasternak met Rosalia Kauffmann in Odessa he was immediately won over by her charm and fascinated by her ability as a pianist. Soon they were strong friends. There were two reasons why Leonid hesitated on the brink of marriage. First, whereas he was an almost unrecognised painter, Rosa was – as will be shown – already a concert pianist whose fame was rapidly spreading. Secondly, Leonid's high-minded determination to pursue the artistic life regardless of personal happiness made him doubt if the sort of resolve which the painter needed to succeed, which had helped him to overcome parental opposition, could blend with family life and the every-day worries connected with it. His inborn sense of responsibility and sensitivity of character brooding on this problem prompted a nervous illness which lasted about a year.

Recovered, Pasternak decided to go to Moscow, to give him time to think the matter over further. This year – 1888 – saw the completion of his first really successful picture, the big *genre* canvas *A Letter from Home*. It became a talking point among collectors and painters in Moscow, and Pasternak was overnight thrust into the forefront of Russian *avant-garde* painters. Reassured by this triumph he returned to Odessa and in 1889 married Rosa.

For Rosa this inevitably meant altering the course of her life. Experience gradually taught her that it was impossible to combine the exacting life of a concert pianist and teacher at the Odessa Conservatoire with that of an over-conscientious wife and mother. So her public appearances became less and less frequent, although music continued to be a vital feature of the Pasternak household. On the relatively few occasions in later years when she did play to an audience her brilliant technique and the quality of her interpretation were immediately realised.

Without the aid of recordings it is almost impossible to convey to a later generation a true assessment of a musician's gifts or achievements. An outline of Rosa's career before she met her husband is, however, vital to an appreciation of

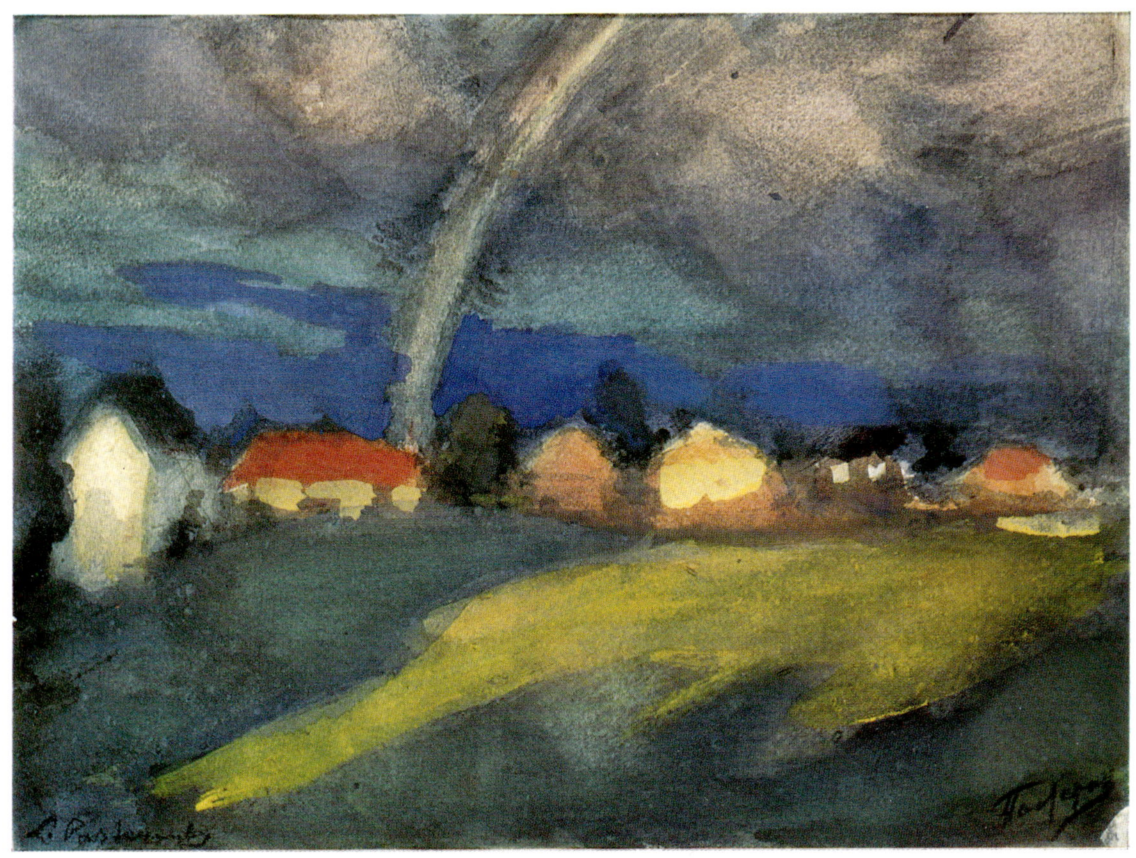

Rainbow over a Field, 1928, watercolour, 18 × 25 cm.

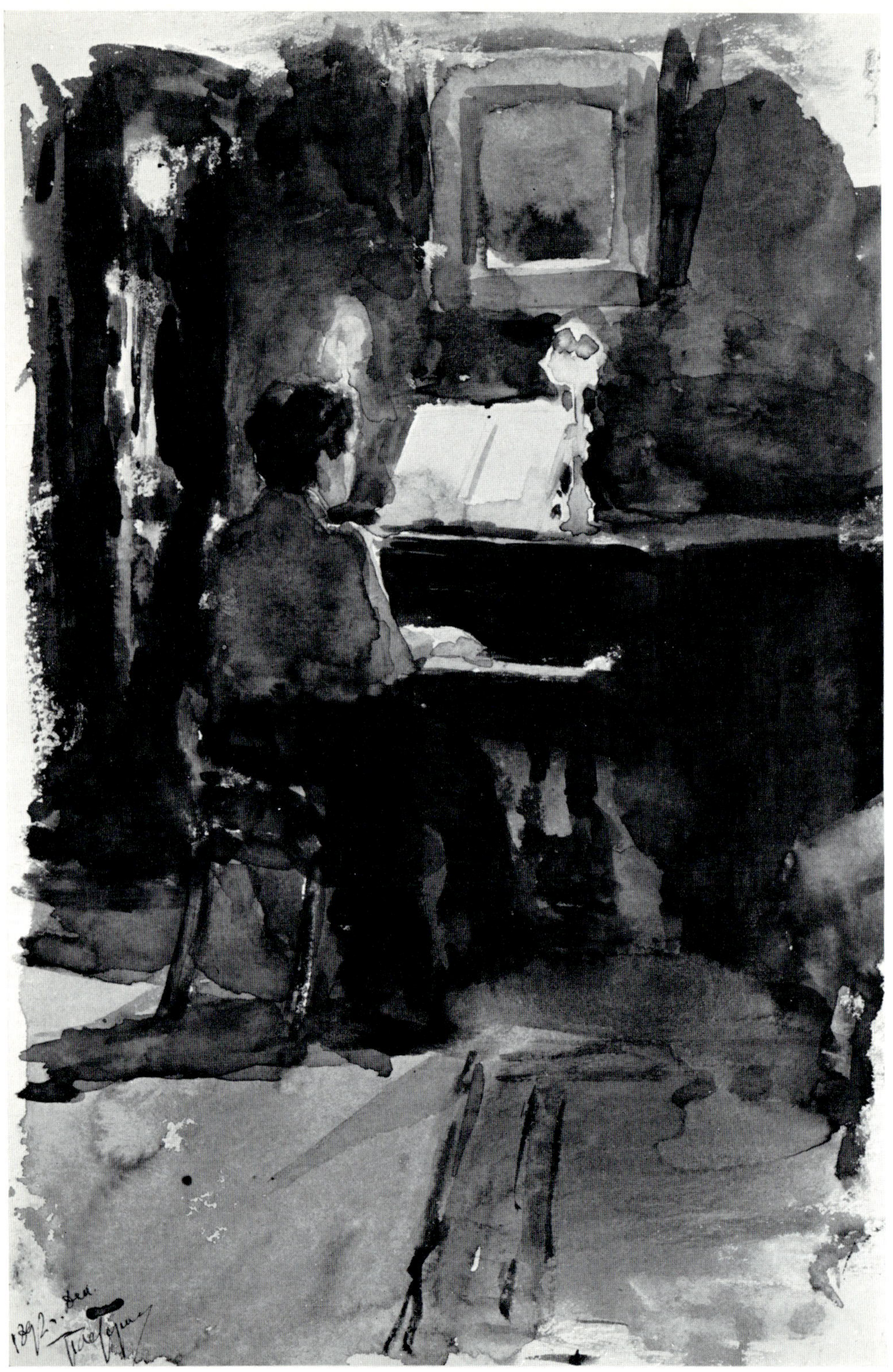

Rosa Pasternak at the Piano, 1892, watercolour, 28 × 19 cm.

Leonid's anxiety about what marriage would cost her and of her role in the formation of the Pasternak household. Lydia Pasternak, whilst admitting that 'the reader will decide I am biased as a daughter', asserts that 'in the whole of my life I have heard nobody play as she did, not even the greatest. There may be a greater virtuoso, a more brilliant performer, but no-one with deeper penetration, something indefinable . . . . Every time I listen to a great pianist on a record, on the radio, at a live concert, I am ready and longing to relive this, to be able to point out to my children: "This is how she would have played it" . . . . But it is like the mirror's answer in *Snow White*, again and again: yes, incredible, wonderful, superb, overwhelming; but . . . not *quite* like her'.

The Pasternaks' younger daughter has no doubts about the price paid by Rosa in abandoning her musical career, and interestingly comments that 'although she never gave up her art (our house, our lives were steeped in music) I cannot help feeling that her sacrifice was too great, and that it would have been better if we had not been born. But maybe it was vindicated by the existence of Boris'.[4] It is clear from Boris' autobiographical writings how important music was to him as a young man. Later he wrote: 'Much, if not everything, I owe to my father, the Academician L. Pasternak, and to my mother, a magnificent pianist'.[5]

The means by which the researcher today is able to trace the course of Rosa Kauffmann's early life is another indication of the impact she had made. Her elder daughter, Josephine, once met a contemporary and close friend of her mother, then living in Germany, who had clear memories of Rosa and who had for many years carefully saved innumerable press cuttings which covered much of her career.

Rosa was born in Odessa in 1867, the daughter of a soda-water manufacturer, a self-taught but unassertive man. By contrast his wife was an energetic, decisive woman, and it was probably she who decided that Rosa would be a singer. She had herself sung in her youth, and Rosa's sister became a professional singer. Rosa started to speak clearly when she was only one year old, at the age of two began picking up tunes easily, and before long was entertaining visitors to the house.

The course of Rosa's musical career was changed when her father bought an old piano. On this Rosa, unaided, at once tried to play the melodies she had learned to sing. After experimenting for some time she succeeded, and henceforth spent hours at the piano, picking out tunes and trying to give them a suitable accompaniment. A year later a cousin staying with the Kauffmanns was given piano tuition, during which Rosa, now five years old, used to stay in the room listening and watching intently or, if she did not wish to be observed, would hide under the piano itself. When the teacher eventually asked her why she was so curious, Rosa's answer was to jump onto the piano stool and triumphantly play through several pieces.

Told by her parents that Rosa had never had a single lesson, the teacher suggested that they arrange regular tuition for her. The opportunity occurred when a musician friend of the Kauffmanns heard about Rosa's debut. Asked if she liked sweets and promised heaps of them if she would play, Rosa sailed through her whole repertoire. The musician friend insisted on teaching Rosa free, and in her eighth year she gave her first public recital. It was a triumph – although in later years Rosa said that at first she had been so bewildered on the platform that she had failed to notice the grand piano.

Odessa now showed a serious interest in the child prodigy, and a better piano was bought for her. When in 1877 she gave her second public concert, the hall was packed and all the music critics were present. After another triumph the small child was borne out of the hall by enthusiastic fans, who nicknamed her 'Mozart in skirts'. An important outcome was that Professor Ignaz Tedesco, sometimes called 'the Hannibal of octaves', one of Russia's finest teachers and a musician with an international reputation, took over her tuition. Tedesco's regime was a strict one, although he and his wife became very fond of Rosa, drawing her parents' attention to her frail health and poor eyesight.

From 1880 Rosa, then aged 13, became the idol of concert audiences during her tours through southern Russia, especially Kiev, which had heard the best European pianists. One critic writes: 'At the fixed time punctually there appeared on the platform a girl modestly dressed; extremely sympathetic and (which is a rarity among precocious talents fed with flatteries) quite unpretentious and natural. Without gesture she sat at the grand piano and began to play Beethoven's sonata in C-major. With the first chord all my prejudices against "an infant prodigy" vanished . . . .'

This critic's comments recalled those of another, writing several years earlier, who had at first been dismayed at the thought of a programme of Mozart, Chopin, Pergolesi and Scarlatti being tackled by an orchestra accompanying a child of 10. Yet he had to admit that: 'With every single chord our astonishment grew. With closed eyes one could imagine that an experienced pianist was playing, not the small thin girl with short hair, a pallid face and dark, sparkling eyes. . . How much of her health she must have forfeited.'

A significant event in Rosa's musical career was her meeting with composer and pianist Anton Rubinstein in 1881, during his visit to Odessa. Learning about Rosa's ability, he asked to hear her play. After he had heard her in Beethoven, Chopin, Handel and Liszt he recommended that she go to Moscow and St. Petersburg to play and to further her musical education. In November 1881 she left on a concert tour that included Kiev, Kharkov and Poltava. In Moscow, through Rubinstein, Rosa and her mother met a wealthy lady landowner, well-known as a patron of young talents, who insisted that she should pay for Rosa to go to St. Petersburg. The outcome was that Rosa – still a rather timid, retiring child – met staff at the Conservatoire and took part in concerts with Karl Davidov and Pablo de Sarasate. A group of financiers came forward at this

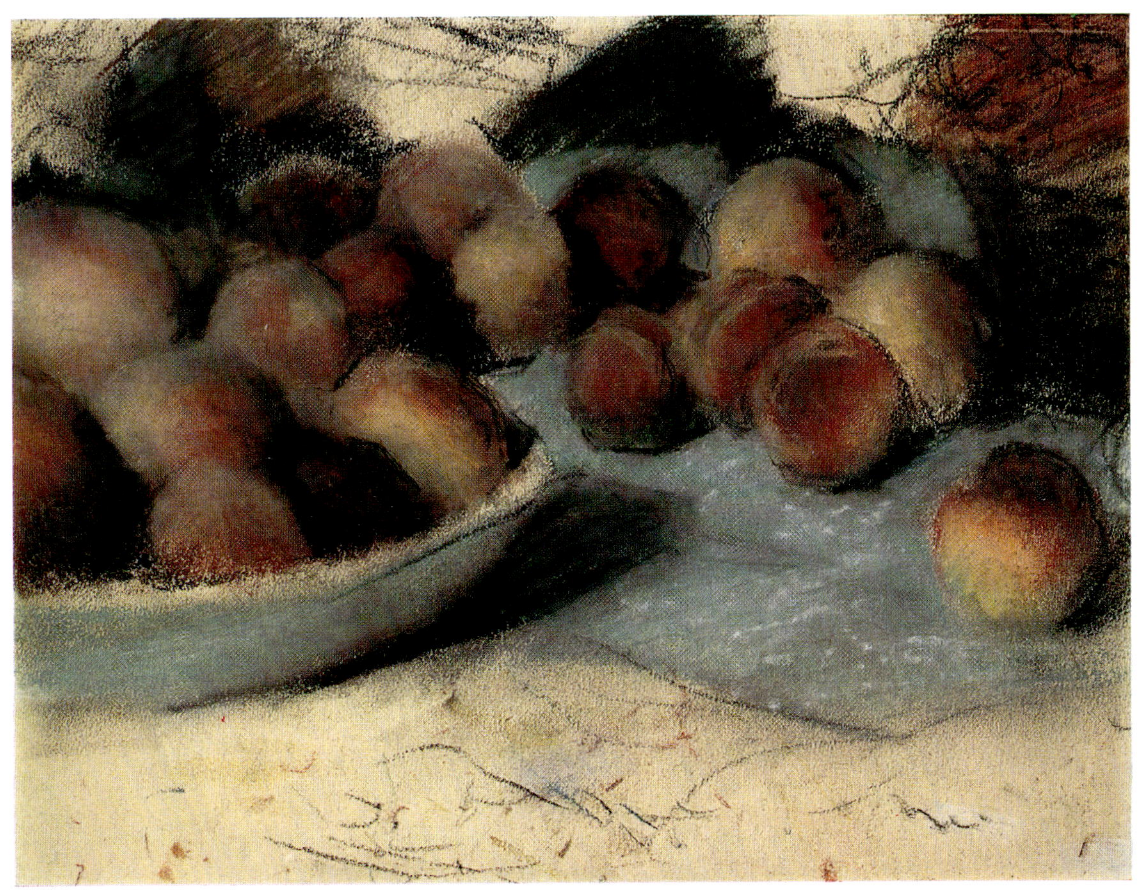

Still Life – Peaches, c.1930, pastel on paper, 28 × 31 cm.

point and themselves offered to fund her musical education.

All this unusual strain and nervous excitement undermined Rosa's resistance to the harsh northern climate. Leaving a concert she caught cold, a condition that was aggravated by an attack of typhus, and she became dangerously ill. Her concerts had to be cancelled. It took her two months to recover sufficiently to travel and another two months in a sanatorium in the Crimea before she was allowed to return to work. She resumed her studies with Tedesco, who eventually declared that she was ready for a concert tour abroad. Rosa left Odessa on 30 October 1882, and on 1 November came news of Tedesco's death.

The death of her teacher was such a shock to Rosa that she became ill once more, and the tour abroad was cancelled. It was St. Petersburg all over again: just as a big step forward in her career was about to be made fate seemed to hold her back. In an unpublished memoir of her mother, Josephine Pasternak suggests that these two shocks in adolescence may have made Rosa suspicious of fame. Fame seemed to demand sacrifices, to require the cultivation of a hardness and determination which would have been unacceptable to her. Difficult as it is to speculate, Josephine Pasternak thinks that the decision Rosa made several years later to jettison her career for a normal family life may have stemmed from these early set-backs and the misery that surrounded them.

The year after Tedesco's death saw Rosa return to the concert platform, however, and there was still a period of significant advancement before her. Following a score of successful recitals in all the big Russian and Polish cities in 1883, Rosa took Rubinstein's advice and went to Vienna to study under the pianist Theodor Leschetitzky. From the way she spoke of him in later life, Leschetitzky clearly had more influence on Rosa Kauffmann than any other teacher.

Leschetitzky was used to a stream of aspirant pupils wishing to join him in Vienna and was very particular which he accepted. Rosa was only 16 when she went to Vienna, yet the reception for the recital she gave only a fortnight after arriving in this European musical capital was a convincing recommendation. The critics enthused about her – she had 'surpassed our most audacious expectations', had given a 'masterly performance', and one claimed that 'with her interpretation of some pieces she excelled Liszt and Rubinstein'.

Rosa studied in Vienna for a couple of years. After this she returned to Odessa, where, at 19, she became teacher for advanced piano classes in the Conservatoire. Then in 1889 she married Leonid Pasternak and her life changed its course entirely. They moved to Moscow, which was to be their home for 30 years.

Early Success in Moscow

When Leonid Pasternak arrived in Moscow with his wife he was not entirely unknown. The success of his large *genre* canvas *A Letter from Home* in 1888 had, as already mentioned, put him in the vanguard of young Russian painters.

The picture had been a talking point in artistic circles in Moscow in 1888

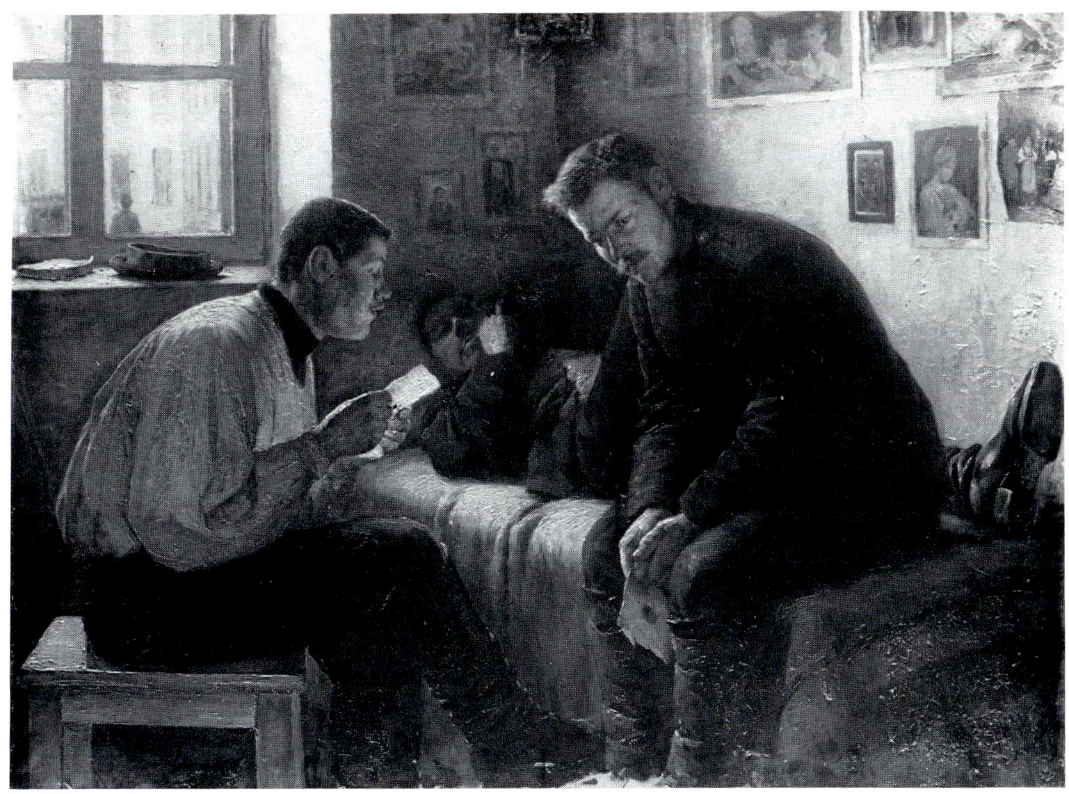

A Letter from Home, 1889, oil on canvas, 110 × 152 cm.

because of its subject, the way it was painted and the way it was purchased. Pasternak was fortunate to have it accepted by the powerful *Peredvizhniki* exhibiting society, the Wanderers. Before it was even hung in the exhibition, however, the notable collector Pavel Tretyakov had visited Pasternak in his furnished room and bought the picture off the easel for the high price of 2,000 gold roubles. This meant that a space was guaranteed it in Tretyakov's own gallery, the first museum in Russia to be devoted solely to native painting. The Tretyakov collection was given to Moscow in 1892 and still bears its founder's name.

Pasternak was warned that this instant success might well have its disadvantages, that, because of the more conservative of the Wanderers, it would cost him dear. When in 1889 Pasternak submitted another painting for the Wanderers show it was turned down, a bitter blow in a year when he and Rosa were trying to establish themselves in Moscow.

A Letter from Home had a number of novel features. Until its appearance, *genre* canvases at Wanderers shows had been noticeably smaller than the historical pictures which flanked them. Again, these big figures in Pasternak's painting were clearly people, the artist was obviously interested in making them seem real.

A contemporary critic comments: 'In the mouths of the men and women he draws one feels there are tongues, and on his flower pieces it seems as if the sun is always shining.'[6] Although not an Impressionist picture, there are in *A Letter from Home* – a copy of which is owned by Pasternak's daughter Josephine at Oxford – hints of that lightness of palette which had all but lured the artist to Paris whilst he was still at Munich.

A soft, dusty pink – a colour familiar to many of Pasternak's canvases – predominates in this simple yet memorable picture of three young soldiers off-duty in barracks. One sits on a wooden stool intently reading aloud the letter, sunlight striking his shirtsleeved shoulders through the window behind. A second man faces him sitting on the edge of a bed, head cocked forward, eyes cast down, intent on catching every word. The owner of the bed lies full length behind him, his tunic undone, a cigarette in his mouth and supported by his right hand, the left arm supporting his head, more of an onlooker than a participant. Behind them on the wall are hazy, pinned-up pictures, including one of the royal family.

Pasternak was to achieve his ambition of a visit to Paris in 1889, where he was able to admire the work of Impressionists in the original rather than in reproduction. It was about now that he became acquainted with Vassily Polenov, by that time in his mid-forties, an influential painter, teacher and archaeologist. By the time that Pasternak met him Polenov, his wife and his sister, the painter Elena Polenova, had become identified with the Abramtsevo colony, which had done so much to revive interest in traditional Russian art and artefacts. Polenov was a member of the Wanderers and an established professor at the Moscow School of Painting, Sculpture and Architecture to which Pasternak had unsuccessfully sought entry.

Polenov was a valuable contact for Pasternak. He had among his friends such important painters as Ilya Repin and was in touch with developments in European art. He was more understanding of these than most of his fellow Wanderers and as a Moscow School professor was noted for his liberal attitude. Polenov encouraged such *avant-garde* artists as Isaac Levitan, who brought a new creative expression to Russian landscape painting, and Konstantin Korovin, a pioneer Russian Impressionist. Pasternak and Polenov were always to have great regard for each other. Polenov admired the younger man's straightforwardness and dislike for artistic intrigue; Pasternak in his reminiscences recalled fondly the cordial atmosphere of the Polenov household.

The early 1890's saw Pasternak's reputation as a painter grow, and his talent develop. In 1893 the Wanderers accepted his painting *The Débutante*, Tolstoy's interest in which led to their friendship. Pasternak began to experiment with the representation of artificial light in his pictures, as in his small canvas *Prayer of the Blind Children* and later in his famous *Tolstoy with his Family*. It was this lamplight scene which years later was to arrest Sir Alfred Munnings' attention during his tours of the European galleries.

By the time that he painted *Students Before the Examinations*, of 1895, Pasternak's work had become distinctly Impressionist, recalling traits in *A Letter from Home*. As Carl Meissner was to comment in a 1932 appreciation of the artist: 'Both pictures are already constructed with great mastery and continue in an original yet quite organic way the profoundly Russian tradition of a kind of painting which does not tell a "story", but creates a state of mind, making us understand the spirit of the Russian people. This is not *l'art pour l'art* but an art which is very deeply rooted in existence, in life.'[7]

Meissner also points out that Pasternak, 'now an assured master of Impressionist drawings, was the first to take illustration seriously in Russia'. Reference has already been made to the money Pasternak earned as a schoolboy and as a student from this activity, contributing to humorous periodicals, such as *The Wasp*, *The Bee* and *The Lighthouse*. Later on he drew for the Moscow magazine *Light and Shade*.

It was for this that he illustrated Chekhov's one-act study *Kalchas, The Swan Song*. Pasternak could not have read the play attentively before starting work. He knew that he had to draw one character, the old prompter Nikita Ivanich, and as he was one of the theatrical fraternity Pasternak depicted him clean-shaven. Chekhov, however, had imagined Ivanich with a beard, but when he saw Pasternak's drawing he liked it so much that he changed his conception of the character. It was an episode similar to one that would take place during the illustrating of Tolstoy's novel *Resurrection*, when the author actually amended the text to accommodate a Pasternak drawing.

Mention should also be made of Pasternak's connection with *The Artist*, a periodical covering art, literature and the theatre and containing black-and-white drawings, which thrived in the early 1890's. When the magazine was started up the editor was keen to get Pasternak's work and wrote inviting him to contribute. Pasternak sent off a batch of drawings, but they were returned by the editor's assistant as unsuitable. When the editor heard of this he made the assistant write another letter immediately to Pasternak, apologising, saying that he would take anything he had and, moreover, offering him the position of art editor. Thus Pasternak was put in a position to cultivate draughtsmen of talent, and it is worth noting here that at least one contemporary, the Symbolist poet Konstantin Balmont, considered *The Artist* to be the precursor of the *World of Art* magazine, so important in the late 1890's. Eventually, however, a change in *The Artist*'s policy compelled Pasternak to give up the post of art editor.

It was not surprising that when Pasternak arrived in Moscow with his wife, collectors had jostled with one another to buy drawings by the rising young illustrator and painter. Those charcoal drawings which Herterich had left un-corrected at Munich were so accomplished that when they were exhibited at the Moscow Society of Art Lovers exhibition, Pavel Tretyakov – who had purchased *A Letter from Home* – and Sergei Shchukin were both buyers. Mention has already been made of pioneer work by Tretyakov in founding the first museum of solely Russian art. Shchukin – one of several collector-brothers – was important in that he established, from the second half of the 1890's, an extraordinary collection of French Impressionist and Post-Impressionist works in his Moscow house. Association with such collectors and collections was of great importance to Pasternak's career.

In his reminiscences Pasternak gives a prominent place to the development of sound draughtsmanship. When he arrived in Moscow in the late 1880's he was appalled at the low standard achieved at the time in the graphic arts, and not surprisingly there was little public interest in them. The art of reproduction – lithographs, etchings, engravings, and so on – reflected the preoccupation with narrative content and message found in most Russian painting. Pasternak shows how he fostered an interest in draughtsmanship – stressing the importance of mastering the forms of the human body and other objects – and quotes Michelangelo, Delacroix and Ingres in support of his ideas. Pasternak emphasises drawing's decisive role not only in the graphic arts and in painting but also in sculpture and even architecture. He says that it is not enough to develop fidelity to an immovable object; such soulless copying would be no better than a lifeless photograph. It is essential to master drawing from life, and especially things in movement.

Those who knew Pasternak recall that this theory was constantly put into practice by him. His view was that perfection can only be obtained by constant observation and training of the eye and hand. He was rarely without a brush or pencil in hand or nearby. In nursery, concert hall or meeting his little sketchbook would be ready. Fellow-artists remarked on his ability to 'catch things in flight', to capture those almost imperceptible impressions of motion, of animate objects which 'already are not there a moment later'.

Pasternak maintains that such swiftness is essential to the painting of the portrait, which he considers the highest form of art. This demands not only dexterity, however, but a special flair in the artist for divining instantly what is most characteristic of the subject. So that even a sketch conveying a first general impression will contain the essential 'something' in a person which is unrepeatable, peculiar to him.

This ability is well illustrated in the small sketches that Pasternak was to do of Tolstoy, such as those of him working in the fields. His sketches of children also exemplify his gifts and insight. Pasternak held that 'the nursery is the best exercise for one who wants to master the moving model'. So the comment by Valentin Serov on seeing some of these nursery sketches: 'You have mastered the child' was especially appreciated by Pasternak, coming as it did from a fine draughtsman and portrait painter.

The circle of painters and musicians known to the Pasternaks in Moscow widened. In the first years of their married life Rosa used to give private musical

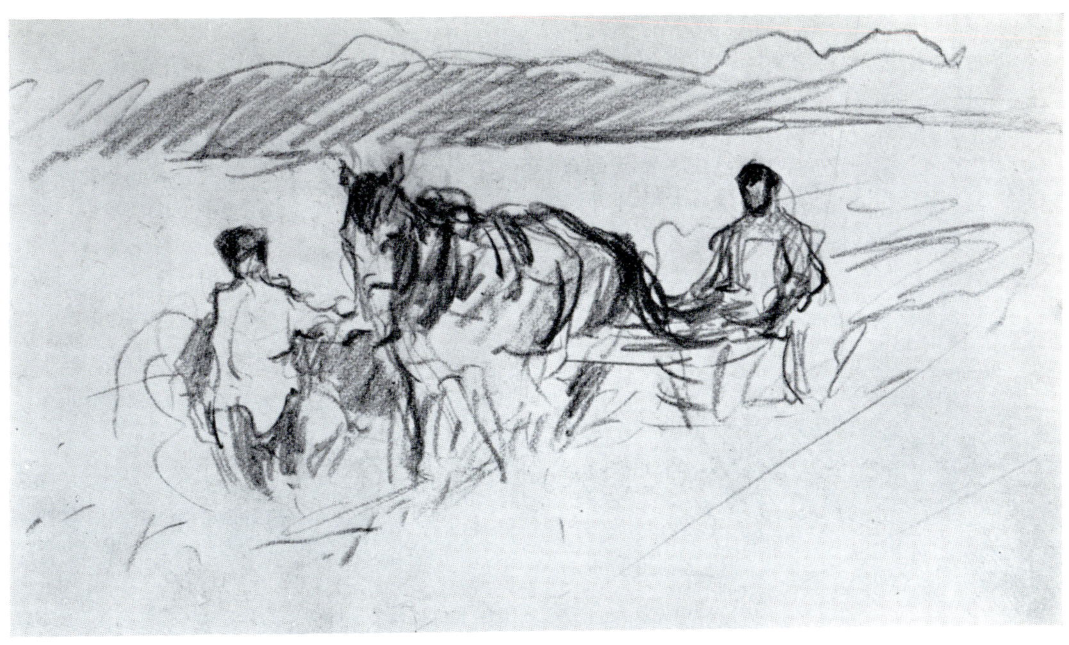

Horse and Two Figures, from a sketchbook, early 1900's, charcoal, 10·5 × 18 cm.

tuition, although this became burdensome when the family became bigger. Boris, the eldest of the four children, was born in 1890. In a few cases Rosa continued to give lessons, notably to advanced students at the Moscow Conservatoire. The Pasternaks' painter-friends covered a wide range. On the one hand there was Nikolay Nikolayevich Gué, noted for his religious and historic scenes, a veteran member of the Wanderers and subscribing to that group's belief that art should explain life and comment on it. Gué thought highly of Pasternak and even called him his successor, a remark which caused the subject some puzzlement, much as he was flattered. On the other hand, the younger painter-friends of Pasternak, such as Serov and Vrubel, were conscious of developments abroad and were already questioning the Wanderers' ideals.

An early period of material hardship in Moscow came to an end for the Pasternaks when Leonid opened his own school. The success of his paintings, Pasternak's reputation as a draughtsman – spread through collectors such as Tretyakov and Shchukin – and his acquaintance with the Polenov circle guaranteed that the school would become widely known. Even Ilya Repin, one of the most distinguished of the Wanderers and the teacher of Serov, sent pupils to Pasternak. Until his death in 1930 Repin was to remain a close friend of Pasternak, corresponding with the younger artist when he was living in Germany. The friendship and support of Repin was of enormous value during the early part of Pasternak's career. Repin considered Pasternak one of Russia's most promising young painters, and when Repin on one occasion staged his own exhibition of new talent he made a point of including Pasternak's work.

Meets Tolstoy and Joins the Moscow School

'Two dates in the early '90's were of great significance to me: '93 – my meeting with Tolstoy, '94 – my joining the teaching staff of the School of Painting, Sculpture and Architecture,' Pasternak writes in his reminiscences. The friendship with Tolstoy was to enrich Pasternak's life and work for many years until, in 1910, he was summoned by Countess Tolstoy to paint the Count on his deathbed.

Pasternak had desired a meeting with Tolstoy some time before it occurred. There was a practical reason for this. In the autumn of 1892 a representative of the periodical *The North* travelled from St. Petersburg to assemble artists to illustrate Tolstoy's already famous *War and Peace*, which was to be given as free supplements to subscribers. Each artist was to choose some scenes and to provide watercolours of them. Pasternak eagerly accepted the commission, for it was his first chance to attempt colour illustrations of a work by an author he had revered since his schooldays. He also felt honoured to be considered alongside the three other famous Russian painters *The North* had approached – Ilya Repin, Alexei Kivschenko and Vassily Vereschagin. 'I plunged into the work,' he writes. 'But it was not easy – in fact it was excrutiatingly difficult to choose only four scenes out of the whole book which contained countless other scenes of equal beauty.'[8]

The initial sketches were completed at white heat, but when it came to preparing the final version of the illustrations Pasternak encountered what seemed an insurmountable obstacle. Essential documentary evidence of the Napoleonic invasion featured in *War and Peace* was not to hand. 'Fantastic though it may sound, there was nothing left in Moscow, the chief scene of most of the events of that historic time – no military uniforms, or civilian costumes, or the interiors of that time – nothing of all that is indispensable for a painter whose intention is to paint true to life and to the historic setting.' Such secondary sources as books were not adequate, Pasternak felt.

'There were many things which I could learn only from the author himself. He still lived in Moscow at that time, scarcely half an hour away from my home. With illustrators it is an understandable and natural yearning to show one's pictures to the author and hear his judgment. Even the great Delacroix used to send his *Faust* illustrations to Goethe for his opinion; yet I could not bring myself to approach Tolstoy . . . . To address myself to such a giant I lacked the necessary courage in those days.'

Mention has already been made of Pasternak's picture *The Débutante*, accepted by the Wanderers for their exhibition in 1893. Pasternak explains how his striking full-length canvas of the girl with golden plaits brought him face-to-face with Tolstoy. 'The day before the opening I came to see how it was hung. The big halls of the Moscow Art School, where the *Peredvizhniki* used to have

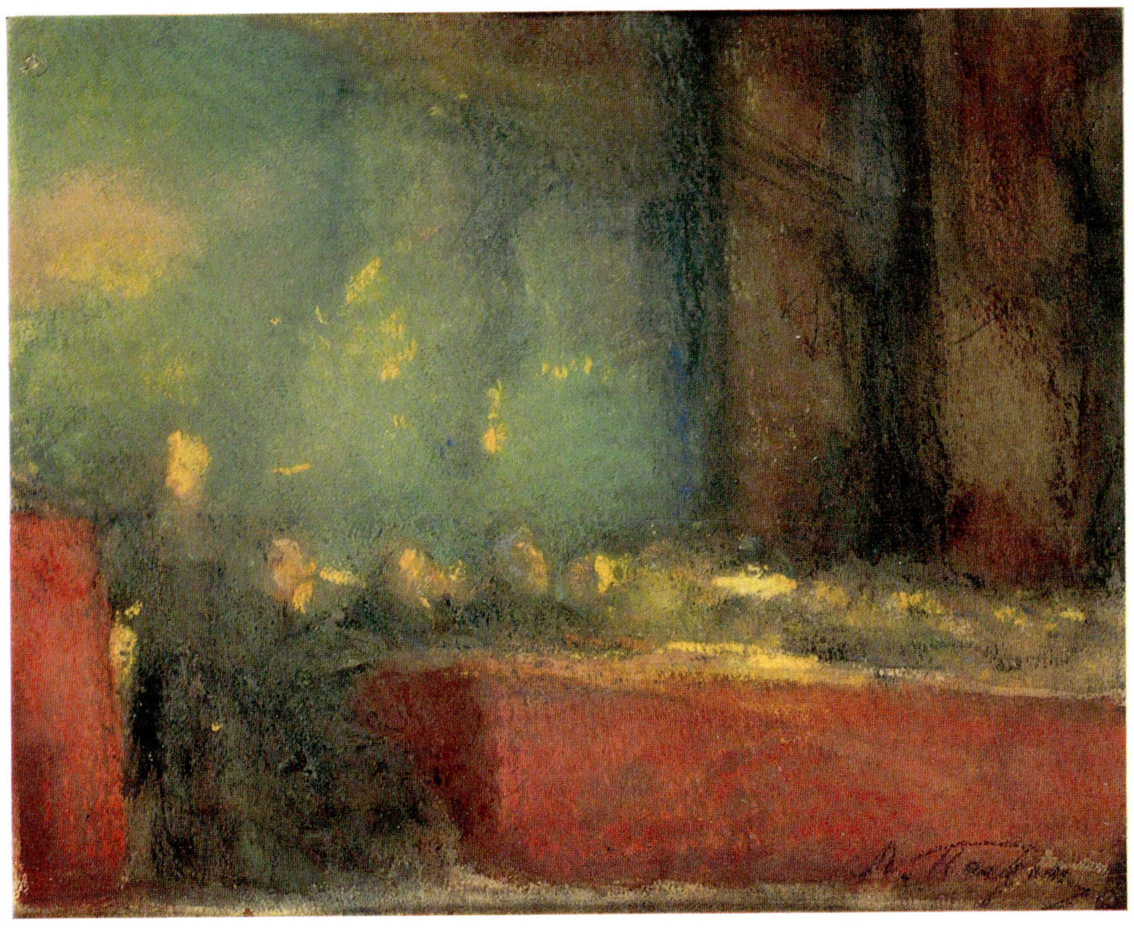

Lenin at the VII All-Russian Meeting of the Soviets, in Moscow, March 1918, pastel sketch on paper, $13 \times 16{\cdot}5$ cm.

their shows, were flooded with spring sunlight. There was the greatest commotion – the sound of hammering, the squeaking of nails being pulled from crates – the usual last-minute rush before the opening of a big exhibition. The senior members in big fur coats stamped around, inspecting the rows of hanging pictures.

'With all this deafening noise going on I was unaware that something very exciting and unexpected was occurring near the entrance. Suddenly when it became quieter I could hear the words: "He's coming straight away."' Tolstoy, it seemed, had been given special permission to view the exhibition in advance to avoid the crowds. There suddenly in the doorway 'stood Leo Tolstoy in his grey blouse with a leather strip for a belt . . . the great author of *War and Peace*. And he did not look intimidating at all. A very lovable, simple, yet dignified old man who seemed to be ill at ease . . . . Despite his sixty-five years he appeared lively, robust, and of great strength of mind and body.'

Pasternak describes how Tolstoy next turned his penetrating gaze towards the paintings. 'He walked, hands in his belt, with a quick, gliding pace, scarcely raising his soles – a manner peculiar to him. He carried his body with ease, and his head was slightly raised, looking straight forward. The viewing began.' Pasternak was later to capture this moment in a masterly drawing. Surrounded by crowds of people admiring the paintings Tolstoy is thrown sharply into profile, his fingers dug into his belt, his bearded chin thrust questioningly and uncompromisingly forward, as if demanding: 'What's *this*? Who's *this* by?'

It was left to R. A. Savitsky, a veteran member of the Wanderers who was an old friend of Pasternak, to escort Tolstoy round the show. 'Unnoticed, at the rear of the group, I tried to catch his words, to hear his opinions,' writes Pasternak. 'Another few paces and he would be in front of my picture! "This is *The Débutante* by a gifted exhibitor, Pasternak"' – scarcely had Savitsky pronounced these words when he was interrupted by Tolstoy's benevolent voice: "Oh, yes, yes, I know him already. I've been following his work . . . ." Savitsky then said: "Then would you allow me to introduce him to you, he is here."'

The circle of painters around Tolstoy broke up, and Pasternak, full of excitement, was pushed forward to meet him. 'Even now I can feel the pleasant warmth and softness of his large, firm hand. With that particular kindness of his, with the exquisite politeness of the Russian higher aristocracy, with his peculiar way of taking in a new acquaintance from top to toe in one glance, Tolstoy said something very flattering to me which in my excitement I could hardly grasp – something about my work which he had seen, such as *A Letter from Home*, and about certain drawings of mine he liked – and all this in the presence of my colleagues, some of whom were not too well disposed toward me!'

Not wishing to detain Tolstoy any longer, Pasternak withdrew into the crowd, overjoyed at his good luck. However, there was a bonus to come, for 'as Tolstoy was leaving the exhibition, I took the opportunity of speaking to him about my illustrations and about my desire to be allowed to show them to him sometime.

"Thank you. But of course. I shall be very pleased. Come next Friday. Come to tea. And by all means, do bring your drawings with you." '

Pasternak's second date of 'great significance' was the 1894 appointment to the Moscow School of Painting. By invitation of the director, Prince A. E. Lvov, Pasternak joined the most exciting centre of art education then existing in Russia. His association with it was to last nearly a quarter of a century, until after the Revolution, enabling Pasternak to influence many younger painters.

The Moscow School when Pasternak arrived was within the jurisdiction of the Petersburg Academy of Art. From his notes we learn that certain reforms there had resulted in Moscow teachers leaving for the Academy. Pasternak was appointed to the *Golovnoi Class* – the life-heads studio – replacing Vladimir Makovsky, a prominent realist painter. Several other young *avant-garde* artists – such as Isaac Levitan and Konstantin Korovin, already mentioned – joined the Moscow School staff with Pasternak.

An *avant-garde* atmosphere was not new in the Moscow School. Founded in 1832 as an art group, it had become a college in 1843 and was amalgamated with the Imperial College of Architecture in 1863. From the start Moscow had stressed the value of open air studies from nature. Eventually its greater liberalism was made evident around mid-century by a complete break with the Petersburg academic tradition of studying from classical plaster casts and prints. It was not surprising that the Russian school of landscape painting developed substantially in Moscow, through artists such as Alexei Savrassov, Polenov and Levitan. From the 1860's the first Moscow students returned as teachers, revitalizing the liberal trend.

Unlike the really radical Moscow elements of the early twentieth century – Larionov, Goncharova, Malevich and Tatlin, with their Cubo-Futurism, Suprematism, Constructivism and other isms – Pasternak and his young colleagues did not seek a complete break with tradition. They respected many of their predecessors. However, their desire to get away from the often tendentious story-picture and to introduce light and colour into their palettes caused their pictures to come under strict scrutiny when placed before the Wanderers' hanging committee, and eventually secession became inevitable.

Pasternak soon became engrossed in his Moscow school duties. 'I devoted myself with ardour and enthusiasm to the task of teaching, which I liked so much, and I came to love the School sincerely. During the time I spent on its staff (almost a quarter of a century), I tried to be useful – to serve it with my experience and knowledge wherever I could, and did so with the greatest of pleasure.' He found himself taking on unpaid chores, such as the organization of the School's library, ordering reproductions of old master paintings, obtaining books and subscribing to Russian and foreign periodicals. All this helped the students to become familiar with artistic developments abroad.

The Russian historians of this period Moleva and Beliutin point out that

Pasternak, Korovin and Serov when teaching at the School 'strove to combine the completion of an academic course, acquainting the student with the latest attainments in Russian and West European art, and preparing him for his own creative work . . . . A special role appertains to Pasternak. "An exceptionally educated and cultured man and artist," writes his pupil Shemiakin, "Pasternak sought to apply the methods and principles of a good West European school." Pasternak always aimed at the broadest possible artistic development of the students,' with whom, as Moleva and Beliutin indicate, he was very popular.[9]

Pasternak's memoirs show that his private work and his teaching duties merged. Determined to overcome the problem of the intermediary craftsman introduced into the various plate-making processes which can distort the artist's intention, Pasternak familiarized himself with the techniques of etching, engraving and lithography and established a special graphics department at the School for the students. Keen to experiment with mixed media and to try to improve the chemistry of his own painting, Pasternak also sought to establish a workshop where tempera, fresco and pigment research might be conducted, but the opposition of more conservatively minded members of staff apparently undermined this.

In his reminiscences Pasternak touches on the abortive plan to establish this workshop at the School. 'In the early '90's, at the time of the "Secessions" abroad and other new artistic societies, an interest developed among young painters in resuscitating the forgotten art of the fresco, and tempera, and a keen desire to wage war on the impermanence of our easel oil-painting technique, the non-durability of factory-produced paints, and so on. There was a revival of forgotten methods. As in the past, painters began to prepare their own canvases, following old Italian and Flemish recipes, to grind their own pigments to avoid darkening and blackening.'

In his own work Pasternak had grown dissatisfied with the type of *genre* painting in oils that had won him success at the Wanderers' shows in the first half of the 1890's. For the various exhibitions that were to draw his work around the end of the nineteenth and the beginning of the twentieth centuries he was working mostly in watercolour, pastel – drawings and sketches, tempera with pastel, and so on. Even when he came to complete two of his more imposing groups, *Staff Meeting at the Moscow School of Painting, Sculpture and Architecture* and *Tolstoy with his Family*, one of his principal works, he chose to employ pastel, in artificial light.

'Very early I experienced the unwieldiness and inflexibility of oil paints in painting portraits, especially of women and children,' he writes, 'and I looked for a more convenient method to quickly work from nature. I succeeded in finding my own technique, a combination of tempera and pastel. Later I had to change to oil painting again, in order to avoid the necessity of putting the pictures under glass – so heavy and unwieldy in transport.' He mentions several life-size and three-quarter-length portraits which he finished in mixed-media and pastel, some

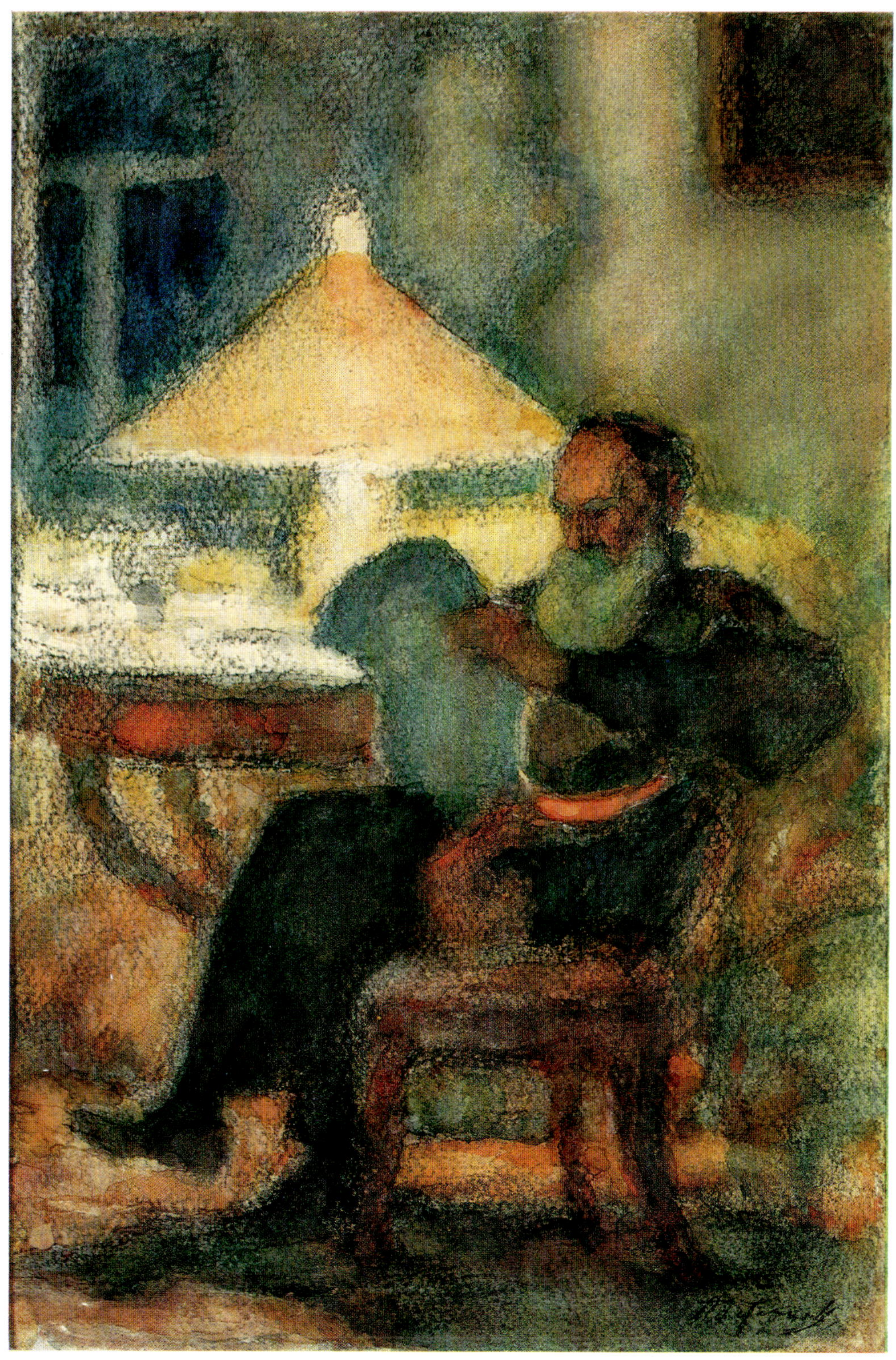

Tolstoy Reading, Yasnaya Polyana, watercolour, 28·5 × 21 cm.

of which were reproduced in the Max Osborn monograph on him, published in 1932.

The establishment of a special graphics department at the Moscow School has already been mentioned as one of Pasternak's most notable early achievements there. Even before he had joined the staff, Pasternak, who years later often paid tribute to his etching teacher I. I. Shishkin, was teaching the skills privately. His own etched, engraved and lithographic work did much to make his name known during the 1890's. One of the most successful ventures that Pasternak was associated with in his early Moscow years was Pyotr Konchalovsky's jubilee illustrated edition of the poet Lermontov's work. Pasternak as well as contributing himself was offered the art directorship and general management of the edition. He was thus able to commission many of the more well-known artists working in Russia, as well as vital new talents such as Mikhail Vrubel, a shrewd choice. Vrubel's work on the edition – his first Moscow commission – was an exciting pointer to an artist who was to inspire the Russian *avant-garde* during the next two decades.

The decision to entrust the Lermontov edition to the young Pasternak was a bold one by Konchalovsky, remembered by Boris in *An Essay in Autobiography* as 'a kindly, shaggy, stooping giant with a deep, toneless voice'. He recalls being taken to visit the family as a small boy, 'their flat, and the pictures on its walls – sketches in pencil, wash and pen-and-ink, by Serov, Vrubel, my father and the brothers Vasnetsov'.[10]

As well as monochrome work Pasternak was closely involved in several ventures calling for the reproduction of watercolours and other paintings employing colour plates. Along with Repin, Serov and other artists he participated in a number of publications, ranging from cheap reproductions for popular consumption to a magnificent edition of the *History of Imperial Hunts*, produced by the state money press.

Another example of Pasternak's illustrative work in the 1890's has already been mentioned – his drawings for *War and Peace*. It was through these that his acquaintance with Tolstoy ripened into friendship. Through them, also, he was invited by the writer to embark on his most ambitious illustrating venture, his drawings for Tolstoy's novel *Resurrection*, which brought Pasternak international recognition.

Illustrating Tolstoy's *Resurrection*

Pasternak eagerly took up that invitation of Tolstoy's to visit him with the *War and Peace* illustrations. But as he waited in Tolstoy's house for the Count to appear the artist's heart beat violently. 'When he saw the portfolio he said in a kindly and jocular tone: "Well, then, let us see quickly what you have brought with you." He moved closer to the lamp and took the first watercolour from my hand. I had depicted Natasha's first ball, with Pierre Besukhov introducing

Prince André to her. In the background, Emperor Alexander I appears in the entrance-way, surrounded by his brilliant suite; the ball is in progress, and in the light of burning chandeliers everything is resplendent with colour. At first Tolstoy said nothing, but turning in the direction of the door he called out loudly: "Tanya, Tanya, come quickly, come!" '[11]

Ironically the daughter who was now called in to appraise Pasternak's work was the same young woman who, several years before, had won the place at the Moscow School of Painting that Pasternak had tried for. Tatyana Lvovna still attended the School when Pasternak met her, although like her sister and mother she was largely engaged in copying her father's manuscripts, proofs and correspondence.

' "But I dreamt of something like that! How marvellous! When I wrote this scene I thought exactly of this kind of illustration. It is excellent, wonderful," ' were Tolstoy's exclamations, as his daughter and Pasternak stood by him. 'He repeated these words over and over again,' writes Pasternak, 'every now and then turning away from the drawing and looking at me attentively. And it was with a singularly gentle intonation that he spoke these words of praise. I must confess it was an unexpected joy to have made this impression on him. He still contemplated the watercolour. Shyness and instinctive embarrassment vanished; no more had I the feeling of being confronted by a grand and severe judge.'

Tolstoy's daughter was equally enthusiastic. Only Pasternak's concern to record the true flavour of the episode can have overcome his normal reticence where his association with Tolstoy was concerned. He was often pressed to talk or write about his relationship with the Count, but would reply: 'My memories of Tolstoy are in my work: portraits, pictures, studies and sketches'. Prodded by his daughters, he eventually wrote down the memoir of Tolstoy now being quoted. Yet even in this, Pasternak tells a curious little story which exemplifies his modesty. Having painted his small canvas *The Reading of the Manuscript*, depicting Tolstoy and the painter N. N. Gué, Pasternak explains that 'in fact it was not Gué but myself to whom he was reading from his newest work. I did not want to perpetuate myself with Tolstoy, and therefore painted him with his old friend instead'.

The inspection of *War and Peace* drawings continued at length. 'Father and daughter examined and talked over all the persons represented in the picture and heaped praise on me as though trying to outdo each other. Tolstoy became more and more interested. "Please show us the next one." I then showed one after the other: *Napoleon and Lavrushka*, *Natasha Visiting the Wounded Prince André* and *The Execution by the French*. With every new picture their interest rose and there was no end to their praise. I very well remember how Tolstoy burst out laughing loudly and merrily when, in my representation of mounted officers in gaily coloured uniforms, in the front of the picture he saw Napoleon in field uniform, stern and grim, listening to the babble of the drunken Lavrushka, riding at his side. Tolstoy was amused by Lavrushka's tipsy countenance and his insolent, high-spirited bearing, contrasting with Napoleon's gravity.'

Encouraged by Tolstoy's friendliness, enthusiasm and gaiety, Pasternak began to ask him detailed questions about costumes and uniforms, to ensure accuracy. 'And then I noticed with surprise that Tolstoy did not remember the text . . . . Tolstoy got so confused that it became clear he had simply forgotten whole scenes from *War and Peace*! We could not help laughing at this.'

The Tolstoy family remained in Moscow until the spring, when they moved to their country home, Yasnaya Polyana. While the Tolstoys were still in Moscow Pasternak and his wife often visited them, then in June 1893 Leonid was invited to Yasnaya Polyana for the first time. Tolstoy's mode of life there was simple. The long, white house was surrounded by an old park and it was there that the Count would walk along the thickly overgrown paths when he was not writing. Alternatively, he might do some manual work on the estate.

It was during this visit that Pasternak began to sketch Tolstoy from life. He had previously only drawn him from memory, not wishing to give the Count any trouble. Thus began the series of depictions of Tolstoy alone, with friends or with his family that have since become so famous and which have been an essential feature of Tolstoy exhibitions.

Pasternak recalls that several days after he arrived at Yasnaya Polyana, one evening when dusk was falling he was talking to Tolstoy's biographer Paul Biriukov when Tolstoy emerged from his study carrying a scythe, an overcoat over his shoulders. 'He invited us to go for a walk with him in the fields . . . . When we came to the meadow, Tolstoy discarded his coat and without breaking off the conversation . . . started mowing. For the first time I began drawing him from life in different postures as he worked. Then, apparently tired, he stopped, threw the coat about his shoulders, took the scythe, and we returned home.' Some of these sketches are still in the collection of the artist's family – Tolstoy with the scythe over his shoulder, honing the blade, swinging it like Levin in *Anna Karenina* to cut grass.

Another significant outcome of this first visit to Yasnaya Polyana was Tolstoy's invitation to Pasternak to hear him read an unpublished work. Biriukov whispered to Pasternak that this was a rare privilege and suggested that the Count would ask Pasternak to supply illustrations. It was, in fact, five years later, in 1898, that Pasternak was asked by Tolstoy's daughter to travel quickly to Yasnaya Polyana to illustrate *Resurrection*, a summons which was to result in 'one of the happiest and most memorable periods of my life'.

Tolstoy was so keen to expedite the illustrations to *Resurrection* that Pasternak had immediately to settle his affairs, wire the Count and take the night train. The urgency arose from the fact that the proceeds from it were to be donated to the Doukhobors, a peasant religious sect that was being persecuted by the Tsarist government. It was Tolstoy who petitioned the Tsar to allow them to emigrate to

Canada. To help the Doukhobors, international magazine and book publication rights were being sought. In Russia the story was to be serialized in the St. Petersburg periodical *Niva*.

When Pasternak arrived it was so early in the morning that everyone was still asleep except Tolstoy, who greeted him on the steps. 'At breakfast, while pouring tea for me and talking about the details of our prospective work, my host was a little tense, perhaps a little impatient too. He spoke of his new story and seemed to be completely carried away by it . . . . At that point *Resurrection* was not yet the long novel in three parts which it later became. It was a comparatively short story, about a third of its eventual length. During the days I read the manuscript, and spent the evenings in Tolstoy's company. Thus passed several unforgettable days.

'But once started, Tolstoy could not stop, and the more he wrote, the more involved the story became. He altered a lot, changed various scenes, left out whole chapters. The end of the work receded farther and farther into the distance.' At one point Pasternak was moved to ask: 'When at last will you banish me to Siberia?', referring to the description of Siberia and the life of the exiles there.

Pasternak records that 'Tolstoy was kind and friendly and valued every sketch, even the smallest. One of my drawings of the governor of the Peter and Paul fortress turned out to have a resemblance to the real governor, whom Tolstoy had in mind when describing *his* Baron Kriegsmut. Sometimes I succeeded in calling forth his genuine, childlike laughter, for instance at the illustration *Zakuska at the Korchagins*, or the drawing with the caption: "Mary, can't you stop just for a minute?" He laughed even more heartily when I showed him *The Judges*. "Oh, but you are even more caustic than I!" he exclaimed. Yet most of the drawings evoked in him a serious mood'.

The story has already been told of how Tchekov changed his conception of a character in his play *The Swan Song* after seeing Pasternak's illustration. A similar situation now arose with Tolstoy and *Resurrection*. 'Once I brought him an illustration I had just completed: *After the Flogging*,' Pasternak recalls. 'Tolstoy, looking at the picture attentively, said again and again, "Very good . . . very good . . . ." His voice broke and a tear crept down his cheek. Suddenly he put his hand to his forehead and exclaimed: "But what have I done! I have wired the publisher to take out this whole chapter! But it does not matter. I will wire him presently to put it back, because the drawing must be included at all costs." ' Pasternak protested, Tolstoy insisted, then he had a simpler idea. ' "At a suitable place in the text I shall insert a reference to the fact that the flogging had taken place, and this will justify the publication of your drawing." And he sent off a wire with this instruction.'

As the writing progressed the first parts of *Resurrection* began to be published. After he had made large drawings to show to Tolstoy, Pasternak copied them and sent the originals to *Niva* magazine, where it came out in 1899. Copies had to be despatched to Paris, London, New York, and other places, as the novel was being published in Europe and America simultaneously. Its success in Russia made publishing history.

In *An Essay in Autobiography* Boris Pasternak recalls that even at the proof stage Tolstoy often made so many alterations that the drawings made for the original version had to be changed. 'Luckily Father's notebooks were filled with sketches of the courtrooms, transit prisons, villages and trains which formed so many of Tolstoy's backgrounds. This stock of living details and the realism which he shared with Tolstoy allowed him to keep close to the text.' Boris also remarks how his father had to work feverishly to meet the deadline and the urgent dispatch work that had to be done on the kitchen table. 'To save time, the drawings were sent off by hand as occasion offered. The guards on the express trains to Petersburg acted as messengers.' The nine-year-old boy's imagination 'was impressed by the sight of a uniformed guard waiting outside our kitchen door, as on a station platform outside a railway carriage. Joiner's glue sizzled on the range. The drawings were hastily sprinkled with fixative and glued on sheets of cardboard, and the parcels, wrapped up, tied and sealed, were handed over to the guard'.[12]

When Pasternak saw reproductions of his illustrations to *Resurrection*, he suddenly felt that all his efforts had been in vain. He writes that, 'in spite of all the praise of the publishers, I was in utter despair because the reproductions were so poor and I could do nothing about it'. But 'a typically Tolstoyan judgment on the value and meaning of a work of art' was the result. 'Tolstoy, seeing my anguish, and wishing to console me said: "Do not take it to heart – you certainly will show the originals of your illustrations in a public exhibition and all will see them and give them their full due. You must remember, Leonid Osipovich, that everything in the world will pass: states and thrones and wealth will perish, our own and our descendants' mortal frames will be forgotten. But, if in our work there is even a grain of true art, it alone will live for ever." '[13]

Family and College Life in Moscow

By the late 1890's, when *Resurrection* was published, the Pasternaks were well established in Moscow, and Leonid was rapidly gaining status not only as an illustrator but as a painter and teacher. Boris' birth in 1890 has already been mentioned. Three years later a brother, Alexander, was born, to be followed by two daughters, Josephine in 1900 and Lydia in 1902.

The Moscow in which Leonid Pasternak and his wife settled in the 1890's was approaching transformation. Whereas St. Petersburg – the official capital since the previous century – had been designed by Italian architects and looked to the West in manners, dress and culture, Moscow at the end of the nineteenth century still had the appearance of a remote, provincial town. Essentially

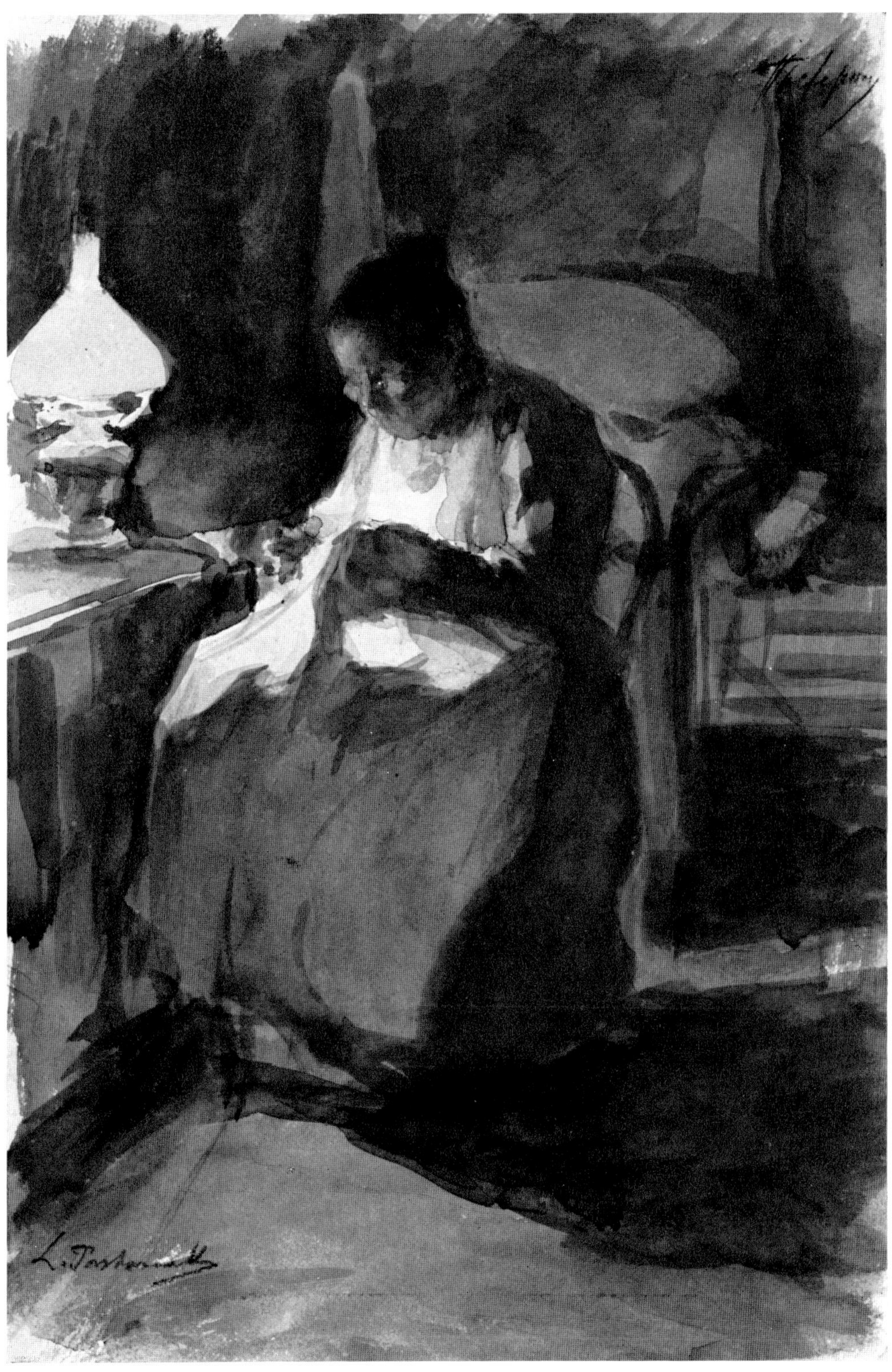

Niania Sewing by Lamplight, 1890's, watercolour, 31 × 24 cm.

Russian rather in character, its people disparaged St. Petersburg attitudes. For Moscow the twentieth century, as Boris Pasternak, remarks, 'changed everything as at the stroke of a magic wand. The city was gripped by the same financial frenzy as were the leading capitals of the world. Tall blocks of offices and flats sprang up overnight in an epidemic of speculative deals'.[14]

The Pasternaks first lived in a flat in a two-storeyed stone house in one of Moscow's poorer districts. It was situated in Oruzheiny Street, above a vaulted archway which led to a yard frequented by coachmen. Opposite was a seminary, nearby were the Znamensky Barracks, and in the vicinity were flea markets, slums and brothels. It was here that Boris was born, into a neighbourhood that he considered 'extremely sordid . . . . You were always being dragged away; you were not supposed to hear this, you were not allowed to know that. But sometimes nannies and wet-nurses wearied of isolation, and then we were surrounded by all sorts of company'.[15]

Wet-nurses stayed longer with Russian children than with those in the West, and were a gay sight when taking their charges out on walks, for they wore national dress. Boris remembers such walks in autumn in the dank, leafy seminary park. When Leonid was still a struggling young painter the nurse would sing a short ditty to Boris:

> 'Sleep my little one, sleep.
> One day, when you are older
> Your father will be able to hire painters
> To do his work for *him*.'

Another nanny, who joined the family a little later, possibly when Alexander was born, is still remembered with great affection by Lydia and Josephine Pasternak. It was she whom Leonid caught in a masterly watercolour. It shows her sewing by lamplight, dumpy, bespectacled and intent as she leans forward better to illuminate her work.

When Boris was small, as mentioned, Leonid was appointed to the staff of the Moscow School of Painting, which provided a contrast to the Pasternaks' previous home. This was a big Italianate building dating from the early years of Catherine the Great, with impressive columns, large curving stairways and rooms lit by chandeliers. It stood in Myasnitskaya, a long, tree-lined street full of well-to-do houses and foreign shops. It was from the School's pillared, semi-circular balcony that the inhabitants were able to witness such events as the funeral procession of Emperor Alexander III and festivities for the coronation of Nicholas II.

Boris remembers such occasions, 'standing near the balustrade, among a crowd of students and professors, my mother held me up in her arms. An abyss opened at her feet . . . . The street waited, holding its breath'. Added to this, 'the spirit of pomp and ceremony was inseparable from the College which was under the aegis of the Ministry of the Imperial Court. The Grand Duke Sergey Alexandrovich was its patron and he came regularly to its exhibitions and its speech days'.[16]

In his reminiscences, Pasternak refers to the drawing soirées at Prince Golitsin's, the brilliant society, the informal atmosphere, the models – society women of outstanding beauty, in evening dress or historical costume. Golitsin's wife was an artist, and the guests – famous painters and some of the host's friends – drew from life. Pasternak describes such an evening, which, because of the presence of several members of the Imperial family, one of whom was a well-known poet, could be called an historical gathering.

Among the high aristocracy there was the Grand Duke Sergei Alexandrovitch, mentioned by Boris, the Tsar's uncle and trustee of the Moscow School. On one occasion he arrived rather late, when the work was already in progress, and Pasternak heard the sound of his spurs, which stopped just behind him. He went on working, pretending not to notice, although the silence continued for so long that he became somewhat uncomfortable.

Evidently the Grand Duke was checking the likeness. It must have been to his satisfaction, because he bought the portrait when it was exhibited. The model was Princess Yussupova, Countess Sumarokova-Elston, a woman of exceptional charm, known in court circles as 'The Radiance'. Pasternak thoroughly observed the Grand Duke's appearance later that evening and back home drew him from memory. This lifelike drawing – indicating the subject's stiff bearing, sternness, and so on – was circulated among Pasternak's friends. Evidently someone took a liking to it, for he never got it back. As they were leaving that memorable evening at the Golitsins' together, Pasternak recalls, Serov remarked to him: 'Some soirée! . . . Would have been worth paying five roubles entrance fee!'

The Pasternaks' flat was on the first floor of an annexe, separate from the main College. It was here that life in the always closely knit family circle assumed a degree of comfort and security that Leonid's parents had always wanted for him, and which they had thought he would only achieve through one of the professions. Pasternak's daughter Josephine remembers, however, that neither her father nor her mother was interested in money matters, but as one of them *had* to look after the family's budget, Leonid entrusted his wife with this tiresome task. The College salary and fees for portraits that accrued to him were handed over to her, and it was to her that he would turn for money even for minor needs, like a tram ride or a visit to the barber. Rosa was now devoting much of her time to her husband and the children, and on occasions the transition from pianist to housewife was not easy. In the Pasternak household a nightmare that Rosa had before one of her now rare concert appearances was used to denote an absurd situation. 'I dreamt', she said in confusion, 'I had to sit down and play – stuffed carp! I didn't know how to begin, it was awful . . . .'

It had been Rosa who had largely organized the mailing and packing of the *Resurrection* drawings, a nerve-racking business calling for meticulous schedule-keeping and great care. She also handled her husband's correspondence, which with his new appointment and portrait work was growing, and helped him at exhibition-times – advising, choosing and in general assisting him in all the preparations. Lydia Pasternak comments about her father: 'For quick decisions, for the practical side of life, for energetic initiative, there was at his side his never-failing source of strength, the throbbing heart of the family: mother.' Sometimes she would have to hurry from the nursery to Leonid's studio to entertain the sitter, for the painter liked his subjects to be animated in conversation, but preferred not to do the talking himself.

Lydia Pasternak gives us a fascinating glimpse of her father's methods. 'When painting a portrait, he would put the easel with the picture next to, and at the level of, the sitter, and would retreat from them to the far corner of the room. From here he would observe and compare the two, completely absorbed in excited concentration, with a smile on his lips, and absent-mindedly muttering encouragement to whatever he was painting, "That's it; yes, yes, right, let's see," etc.; then suddenly, with lightning speed, in one great leap, he would pounce on the portrait, add one or two brush strokes, and return again to his corner, to observe and compare once more. The speed, the ease and decisiveness with which he worked were truly amazing, and in direct contrast with his usual bearing.'[17]

When working well, Pasternak could finish a portrait quickly, which would prompt some droll comments from his fellow-portraitist, Serov. '*My* portrait is only finished when the model leaves town,' he would say. On another occasion he jested: 'When I began the portrait some men across the road were digging the foundations of a house. When I had the preparatory drawing done they had reached the first floor. As I began to paint they were up to the roof. I was still painting when they were packing up their tools and going!'

Rosa's devotion to her husband and family did not keep her entirely from the piano. However, now she preferred smaller, more intimate audiences. It was not surprising that Tolstoy, author of *The Kreutzer Sonata*, liked her to play when the Pasternaks paid one of their long visits to Yasnaya Polyana, and she would make a point of making up a programme from his favourite composers. The entire Tolstoy family would gather to hear her play. After one such visit Countess Tolstoy wrote to Rosa: '. . . even after your departure the house was still filled with the sound of your beautiful music.'[18]

The Pasternaks' Moscow School of Painting flat was another place where Rosa played to the Tolstoys and other friends. Additional musicians might be invited. It was during one such gathering early on in Leonid's friendship with Tolstoy that he made his first, tentative attempt to draw the Count, which later found its way into the Tolstoy Museum. Pasternak's sketch was of Tolstoy 'listening to chamber music (it was Chaikovsky's trio which had just come out and which interested Tolstoy very much). My wife is at the piano, with Professor Grzhimali playing the violin and Professor Brandukov the violincello. I made this sketch

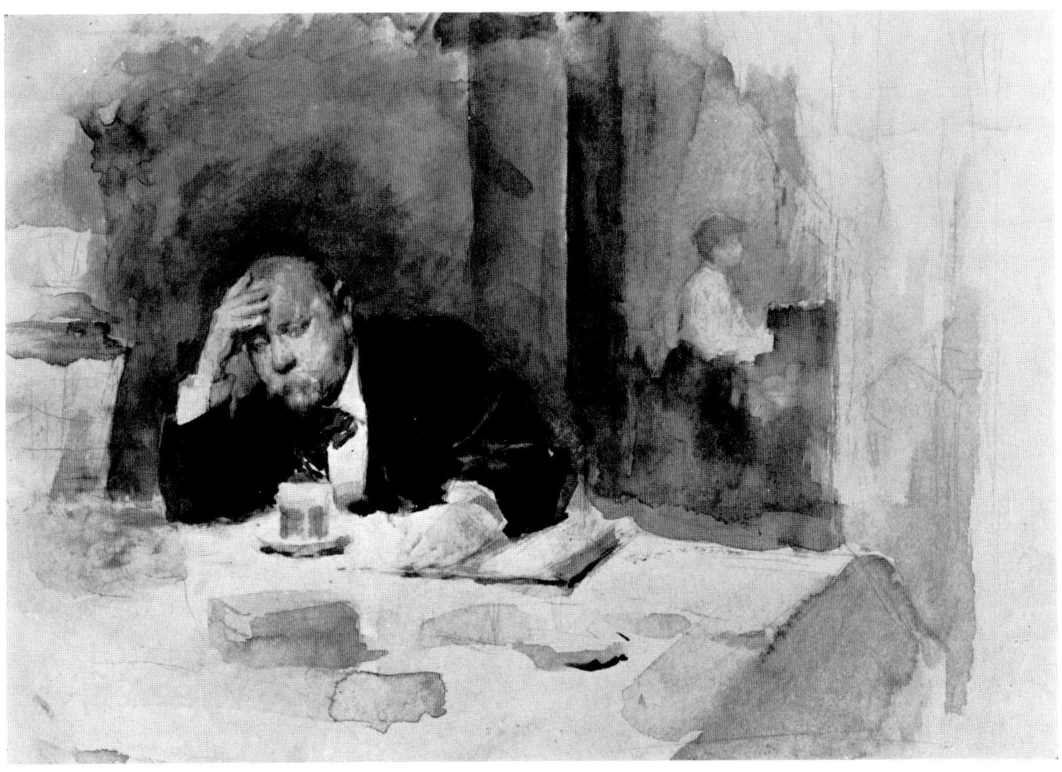

The Artist's Cousin, Karl Pasternak, with Rosa at the Piano, early 1890's, grey washes, 24 × 32 cm.

from memory not from life. I would not have dared to do the latter as any trace of selfish interest must be avoided. I remember how that very evening his two daughters, Mariya and Tatyana, reproached me for this attitude, saying: "But Father would be only too glad to see how you would represent him," '[19] which led to the Yasnaya Polyana mowing sketches previously described.

'I remember that evening perfectly,' Boris Pasternak writes. 'I had been put to bed, but late in the night I was aroused by such a sweet, nostalgic torment as I had not experienced in the same degree before. I cried out and wept in fear and anguish. But the music drowned my cries and it was not until the end of the movement that anyone heard me. Then the curtain which hung across the room, dividing it in two, was pushed aside. My mother came in, bent over me and soon calmed me down. She may have carried me into the drawing-room, or perhaps I only saw it through the open door. The air was filled with cigarette smoke; the candles blinked as if it stung their eyes. They shone on the red varnished wood of the 'cello and of the violin. The piano loomed black. The men were in black frock-coats. Women leaned out of their shoulder-high dresses like flowers out of flower baskets.'[20]

Boris was later to be grateful for his mother's music-teaching, for it enabled him

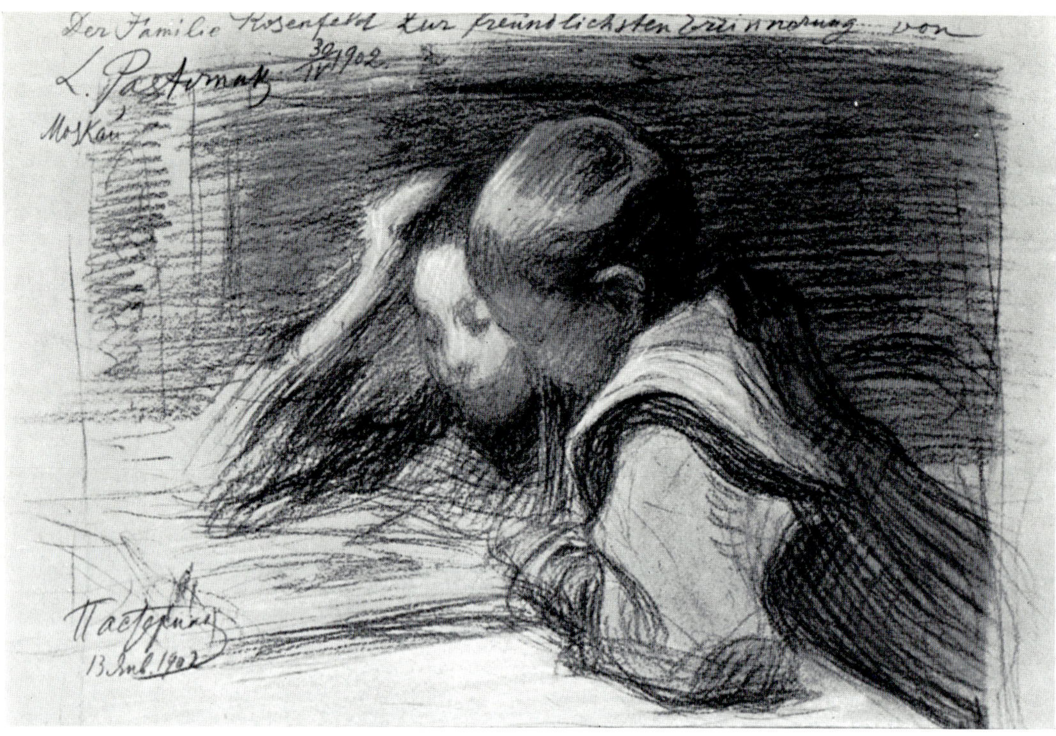

Boris and Alexander in Sailor Suits, 1902, charcoal heightened with white, 23·5 × 31 cm.

to travel abroad when young, like his father. In *Safe Conduct* he tells how 'there
. . . was my mother one morning telling me that she had been putting aside part
of her earnings and housekeeping money, and saved two hundred roubles, and
this she was going to give me, advising me to have a spell abroad . . . . A great deal
of piano-strumming had had to be endured by her to save such a sum'.[21] It
enabled him to visit Germany and Italy, both of which by then Leonid had
travelled through with great interest.

In 1901 the Pasternaks moved again, this time to a new flat within the College.
Because of financial difficulties the authorities had decided to make better use of
space, some of it even being allocated for private construction. The new flat was
converted from two or three classrooms and lecture halls in the main building. It
was at the College that Pasternak did many of the drawings of his children that
were to become so widely reproduced. Some of these have been used to illustrate
An Essay in Autobiography and *Safe Conduct* – for example, the splendid drawing
of Boris in 1898, perched on the edge of a balloon-back chair intently drawing.
He is barefoot, and his concentration is perfectly caught by his father, who shows
the toes of his right foot curling back tight against the calf of his left leg. Then
there is the well-known painting of Boris and his brother Alexander as boys, and
again Boris painted at 16. Although Leonid often drew and painted his elder son,

Boris later wrote to him: 'I think that your best subjects were Tolstoy and Josephine. How you drew them! Your drawings of Josephine were such that she grew up according to them, followed them in her life, developed through them more than through anything else.'[22]

A diversion from Moscow life were the summer visits to the country. Because the School holidays lasted from mid-May to mid-August this was a useful break for Leonid, enabling him to pursue his own work unhindered. Sometimes the Pasternaks would stay in part of a country mansion, sometimes in a *dacha*, a wooden summer house. It was during the summer of 1893 spent in a *dacha* not far from Moscow that they became acquainted with the composer Scriabin and his family. Alexander Pasternak has described how one day he and his brother were exploring the surrounding forest when suddenly 'we heard from far off broken snatches of piano playing. In the proper Red Indian manner, we crept through the thickets towards the sound of the music till we reached its source – and it was marvellous! . . . From that day on we took to establishing ourselves there; from our vantage point we could watch and listen to our hearts' content. The power of the music was such that we were impelled to settle ourselves in our hide-out where, invisible, we could just go on listening.

'One day my father came back in an unusually cheerful mood from his daily walk. He told us laughingly how on his way he had met an extraordinary person coming down the steep hill. This chap was not just walking, but was hopping down, flapping his arms like wings; he seemed about to take off, like an eagle, vulture or other such heavy bird. He might have been thought to be dead drunk. But from his appearance and movements it was clear that he was not, but was more probably an eccentric. At another such meeting a conversation sprang up; though even after this first acquaintance the eccentric flapping and hopping went on. It transpired that he too was a summer visitor, that his *dacha* was in the clearing by the wood (he had pointed to what was almost our hide-out), that he was also a Muscovite, and that his name was Skryabin.'[23]

Leonid Pasternak and Scriabin would walk together. Sometimes Pasternak would draw the composer, on other occasions they would argue about many subjects, Boris always – if uncomprehendingly – on Scriabin's side. On one topic Leonid and the composer profoundly, and significantly, differed. Pasternak had little time for Scriabin's endeavours to mix music with intricate light effects, as in his symphonic poem *Prometheus*. Attempts to fuse art forms were regarded by Pasternak as mere dilettantism which must inevitably dilute a true artist's aims.

By 1905 Pasternak had established his position as one of Russia's leading younger painters and teachers. In that year he, Vrubel, Korovin and Malyutin were elected Members of the Academy of Fine Arts. But when on one occasion he was offered a post at the St. Petersburg Academy he firmly declined. To the painter S. P. Kratchkovsky he writes, 'Belatedly I would like to thank you for . . . your wish to see me in the Academy . . . . However, I would not go there for many reasons: (1) Why should I leave our School which I love with all my heart, and to which I have given my best strength; (2) I don't feel worthy to replace such a great man as Repin; (3) To go to the Academy with its atmosphere – many thanks!'[24]

The Union of Russian Artists

Anyone seriously interested in artistic developments in Europe over, say, the last century can by reading and looking at the right pictures build up a mental reference-system to which new knowledge may gradually be added. This must always be a rather unsatisfactory process, because artists and art movements do not fit into neat pigeon-holes, but it at least offers an instant classification method to help the non-expert with a maze of facts. When this mental filing system – which copes well with Impressionism, Fauvism, Vorticism, Manet, Sickert, Picasso, Cubism, and so on – is consulted not for French, English or German references but Russian ones the pages are invariably almost blank. The names Repin, Serov and Vrubel, the titles Wanderers, World of Art and Union of Russian Artists are not there. They should be, of course, because they are all significant. Without a broad indication of where they stood in relation to contemporary European artists and movements, it is impossible to appreciate Pasternak's place in the important turn-of-the-century period when he was establishing a style and reputation.

The beginnings of Russian painting were hardly original, having started in the Baroque period. It continued during the years of the Empire entirely under the influence of German and French art until, at the beginning of the 1830's, three artists were born who were to create *genre*, landscape and historical pictures with a distinctive national flavour. These were N. N. Gué, already mentioned as an admirer of Pasternak's works, G. Perov and I. I. Shishkin, previously referred to as Pasternak's etching teacher. Gué is obviously familiar with the French manner, but when he paints Russian scenes he becomes original. Perov, who like Gué portrays the important men of his country, has the gift of rendering German *genre* art in a distinctively Russian way. Shishkin's landscapes are serene and vast, their country of origin obvious.

In the 1840's, again in close succession, were born Vladimir Makovsky, whom Pasternak had replaced at the Moscow School in 1894, Vassily Vereschagin, already mentioned in connection with the *War and Peace* illustrations, and Ilya Repin, a great friend of Pasternak, who with other artists helped consolidate the growing Russian autonomous tradition.

This was given a new twist in 1863. In that year a group of 13 pupils and gold medal candidates at the Academy in St. Petersburg, who were disenchanted with the still strongly Western academic flavour of teaching there, refused to paint a picture on the set subject: *Odin in Valhalla*. They formed an artists' co-operative society and with financial aid from Tretyakov, who was eventually to purchase

Pasternak's first major success, *A Letter from Home*, founded in 1870 the *Peredvizhniki*, the Wanderers. This was ultimately to embrace the great names of Russian painting in the last quarter of the nineteenth century – Makovsky, Polenov and Repin being just a few of the members. The Wanderers' revolt against the established artistic order provided the springboard for the modern movement in Russian painting.

The Academy students had made their protest because they believed that art should not be exclusive but popular. They would take painting to the people through travelling exhibitions – hence the name Wanderers. Here they gained moral support from contemporary writers such as Tolstoy and Dostoevsky and the spokesman of their group Nikolai Chernishevsky. It was he who declared that 'The true function of art is to explain life and comment on it', and said that 'Reality is more beautiful than its representation in art'.[25] The Wanderers thus thought that art should become a means of social reform, the debut in Russia of a notion that later found its expression during the Revolution and in the birth of Socialist Realism in the 1930's. Although the Wanderers were concerned with the establishment of a distinctively Russian school of painting, they, in fact, settled in cosmopolitan St. Petersburg, from which their exhibitions went to Moscow and other cities.

By the time that Pasternak was offering *A Letter from Home* to the Wanderers, that body had followed the familiar path of revolutionary groups that endure and become accepted: it had itself become an establishment representing dogmas ripe for challenge. When Pasternak arrived in Moscow at the end of the 1880's the Wanderers had considerably influenced Russian taste with their concept of art as a means of persuasion, the importance they attached to content at the expense of form and their insistence on realism. Rejection by the Wanderers, as Pasternak was to learn in the early 1890's after the instant success of *A Letter from Home*, was a serious setback for a young painter.

Even an artist such as Ilya Repin was prepared to mould his talent to meet the Wanderers' ideals, although by the 1880's these had been refined. In the words of S. Yaremich, biographer of Repin's pupil Vrubel, 'After the crude propaganda style of the men of the sixties, a movement of intellectual nationalism arose which valued a painting for its broad idea and poster-style of expression: in technique an intellectual anonymity was sought . . . . The great talent of Repin was diluted in this dead atmosphere'.[26] In Repin's famous picture *They Did Not Expect Him*, of 1884, a man returns to his home apparently as a poorly dressed prodigal, to a mixed response from his family and servants. There is nothing crude about this canvas, painted by a member of the Wanderers, but it is remote from the Impressionist, non-anecdotal works that Pasternak and a younger generation were to paint within a few years.

Repin completed this picture at Abramtsevo, the artistic centre on an estate near Moscow which had been established in the 1870's by the railway pioneer

Savva Mamontov. Mamontov was typical of the middle-class businessmen and industrialist collectors of Moscow who were to foster the modern movement by their support and purchases, thus complementing the former aristocratic patronage. Several members of the Wanderers, such as Repin and Polenov, who was to befriend Pasternak, as well as later rebels against what that movement represented, notably Serov and Vrubel, were associated with Abramtsevo. It was at Abramtsevo that the famous church was built in the revived medieval Russian style, that the study of icons was fostered and the foundations of a museum of national peasant art were laid. Thus the activities of Abramtsevo went on parallel to the new art movements proper and new ideas about art which clustered in Moscow, in the 1880's, around Polenov and his circle.

Towards the end of the century the younger Moscow painters – Pasternak, Serov, Korovin, Vrubel, Levitan, and so on – and some of the more progressive older ones, who were increasingly dissatisfied with and hampered by the stifling rules of the Wanderers, banded together to create the spearhead of the new movement. This was the 36 Artists group, which very soon evolved into the Union of Russian Artists (*Soyuz Russkikh Khudojnikov*).

The activities of the Union have never been understood or fully appreciated in the West. Thus the modern movement around the turn of the century is identified almost entirely with the *Mir Iskusstva*, St. Petersburg's World of Art group. Unlike the Union, which was a forward-looking, exhibiting association of painters, whose supreme concern was art and the freedom of artistic expression, the World of Art was a mixed art-and-literary society, an exhibiting body, a magazine, and was strongly associated with the theatre and ballet. It involved brilliant organisers and publicists such as Alexander Benois and Sergei Diaghilev.

Benois was the World of Art's intellectual driving-force, whose background in St. Petersburg led him to regard the Wanderers' activities as insular and restrictive. Coming from an artistic family with foreign ancestry and cosmopolitan connections, it was not surprising that the movement he helped to inspire and direct should seek to establish contact with contemporary artistic life. Thus French, German and English painters were represented both in the pages of the *World of Art* magazine and in its exhibitions. Art Nouveau, the Vienna Secessionists, Böcklin and the Munich School and the Nabis – with which the World of Art had much in common – all found favour.

However, the World of Art did not reject all that had been produced in Russia. As Camilla Gray writes in her account of the movement: 'They believed that Russia should not return to the status of a provincial outpost of Western Europe, nor remain the stronghold of an isolated national tradition. Their aim was to create in Russia an essentially international centre which would for the first time contribute to the mainstream of Western culture. To do this they set about restoring contact again with German, French and English ideas, as well as by encouraging an interest in the national heritage, not only that of medieval Russia

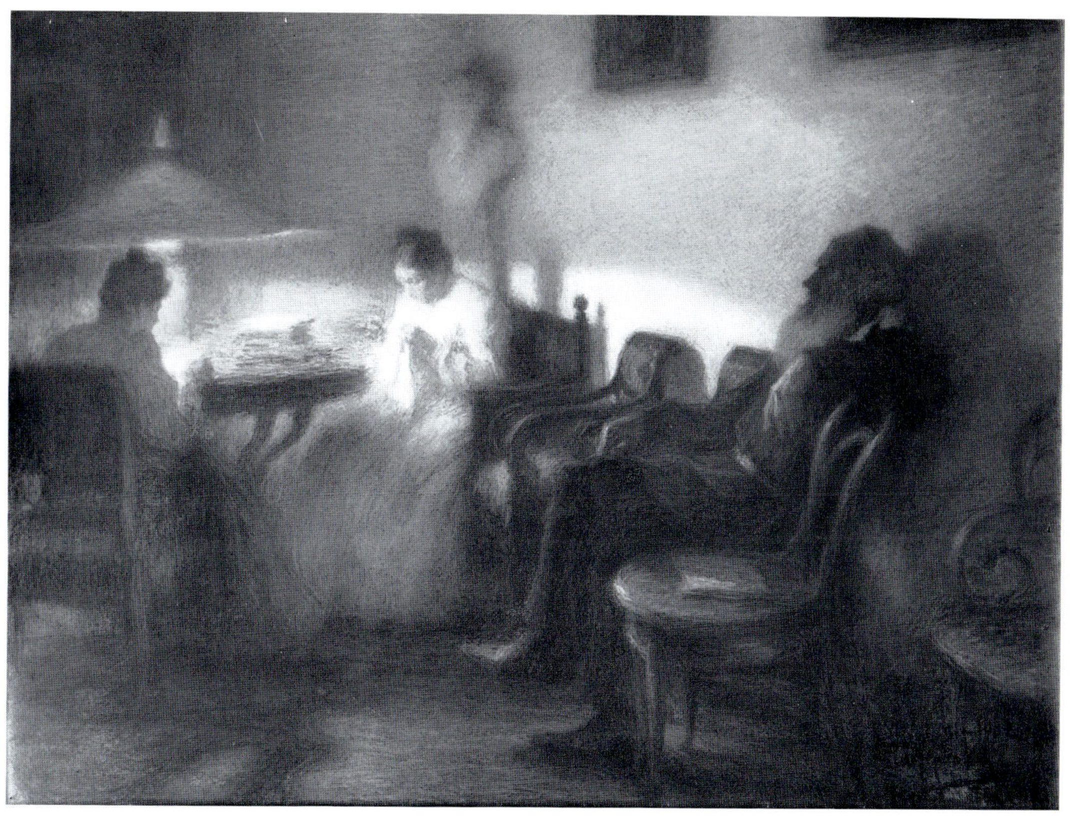

Tolstoy with his Family, 1902, pastel on paper, 58 × 76 cm.

to which the Abramtsevo colony had dedicated themselves, but also to the much neglected art produced under Peter and Catherine the Great which had been completely dismissed by the "Wanderers" as alien.'[27]

Abramtsevo's influence was evident in the first World of Art exhibition, where pottery and embroidery designs from the colony were both shown. But it was Abramtsevo's theatrical pioneering with the use of professional painters to produce sets that was to be its most marked influence on the World of Art. Thereafter, the backcloth became part of an integrated production. It was this concept that Diaghilev was to incorporate later into the Russian Ballet, 'the most significant expression of the "World of Art" movement', in Camilla Gray's opinion.[28] Through his ballet, opera and exhibition activities in Paris in the early years of this century Diaghilev broadcast the World of Art message. Mistakenly, modern Russian art became identified in the West with these theatrical productions and such names as Alexander Benois, Léon Bakst, Mikhail Larionov and Natalia Goncharova. Whereas to most World of Art painters 'the sphere of advertising and publicity was alien', Benois writes in his memoirs, 'Diaghilev was marvellous in it – he was a born master of the art'.[29]

As mentioned previously, several of the Moscow artists bridged the division between Petersburg and Moscow at this period. Serov, for example, collaborated on the *World of Art* magazine, the first issue of which appeared in 1898. He and Korovin were only visiting members of the organization, however. Diaghilev called on Pasternak at his studio on several occasions requesting pictures for World of Art exhibitions, and Pasternak was sufficiently impressed by Diaghilev to contribute. 'For several years I used to show my work at the exhibitions of the *Mir Iskusstva*,' Pasternak writes in his memoirs. 'My pictures were mostly water-colours, pastels, drawings and sketches, and tempera with pastel, a different technique which I was employing at that time.' It was at the World of Art that one of Pasternak's finest pictures was exhibited. 'Five Russian artists had been commissioned by the Luxembourg Museum [in Paris] to paint scenes from Russian life. The painters were Repin, Serov, Korovin, Maliavin and myself. I drew the composition *Tolstoy with his Family* .... Before going to Paris my picture was shown at the *Mir Iskusstva*. The Grand Duke Georgii Aleksandro-vitch saw it and through Diaghilev bought it for the Museum of Alexander III, in Petersburg.' In spite of the Luxembourg's initial approach, Pasternak was glad that his picture remained in Russia.

The seeds of the World of Art movement were sown by the Nevsky Pickwick-ians around 1890. This was a self-education study group established by Benois and schoolfriends with a similar cosmopolitan background at the May College, in St. Petersburg. However, it was not until 1898 that their first World of Art-inspired show was held, the first official exhibition occurring in the following year. What is virtually forgotten today is that a similarly forward-looking art movement was taking place in Moscow in the 1890's. It was also to come to fruition late in the decade and was early in the next century to spawn that much more enduring and catholic exhibiting society, the Union of Russian Artists, of which Pasternak was to be such a prominent member.

Reference has already been made to Pasternak's desire for a lighter palette when studying in Munich. His visit to Paris in 1889, where he was able to appre-ciate Impressionist canvases at first-hand, aggravated his dissatisfaction with aspects of contemporary Russian art. A sketch of his wife playing the piano, completed in 1892, is just one example of his early work that is notably Impres-sionist in treatment. As noted before, the painting *Students Before the Examin-ations*, of 1895, was clearly influenced by what Pasternak had seen in Paris.

The friendship with the artist Vassily Polenov and his sister Elena Polenova also fostered Pasternak's interest in advanced painting outside Russia. As men-tioned earlier, the Polenovs were in touch with European developments (at their house in the 1890's Pasternak would have seen *The Studio*, published in England, as well as other foreign magazines). So it is not surprising that when around 1890 some of the younger Moscow painters such as Pasternak, Korovin and Golovin were mulling over the idea of a more democractic and tolerant exhibiting society to challenge the supremacy of the Wanderers, the Polenovs were in on the idea. 'Events, quite significant for the future, have taken place here, with us, in art circles,' Elena Polenova writes. 'This year, in particular, relations have become very strained between the old and young, between the Wanderers and the Exponents*. . . . Mention was made of forming a separate society. But this is premature – besides, too much time and effort would be taken up by such a venture, which is better employed in creative work.'[30]

Even Repin, by then an established painter, hoped for a new society. Writing from St. Petersburg to Polenova in October 1896, he discusses an exhibition, 'You, V.D. [Vassily Polenov] and Pasternak, whom I have already invited personally, I will welcome as dear guests, and I will place your pictures in the best possible position.'[31] Later that month he writes again: 'Please, I beg you, let me know what your circle of young Moscow artists thinks of the venture . . . . This exhibition will include many things new, interesting, quite unexpected. From the future organization of the society we will try to ban any kind of formalism, of regimentation.'[32]

By this time – 1896 – Pasternak was an established member of the Moscow School of Painting. There he began to share with his colleagues who did not read the language anonymous art reviews that appeared in a small German newspaper, the *Petersburger Herold*. This indicates how aware they were of new influences from every quarter. The *Herold* reviews impressed the Moscow artists by their open-mindedness and lack of partisan bias, for at that time much of Russian critical opinion was still wedded to the outlook of the Wanderers. 'The author of these articles in the *Petersburger Herold* was so conversant with all he was writing about,' explains Pasternak, 'as if he had been a comrade, a participant in the hopes and strivings of the young Russian painters. His judgements and his appraisals were of a very high standard, and therefore carried weight with the authors of the exhibited pictures . . . . I must admit that I personally was very pleased with his assessment of my works . . . mainly because he understood me and caught the essence of my intentions.'

Polenova's letter, Repin's invitation and Pasternak's comments on the *Petersburger Herold* are just a few indications that in the 1890's artistic revolt in Russia was, in fact, begun in Moscow. The Polenova letter was written in the year that Benois met Bakst and Diaghilev became associated with the Pickwickians. Eight years were to pass before the World of Art organized its first exhibition, the first of several that were to take place until 1903.

At the turn of the century a new exhibiting society made its appearance, the Moscow-nurtured group 36 Artists (*Tridtsat' Shest' Khudojnikov*), forerunner of the Union of Russian Artists. 'The formation [of the Union] was preceded by two

---

*The Exponents, or exhibitors, at Wanderers shows had no rights, unlike Members of the Fellowship of the Wanderers.

exhibitions by the group 36 Artists,' explains Y. D. Mintchenkov, in his reminiscences of the period. 'When the Union was founded it was joined by some of the Wanderers who had left the Fellowship of the Wanderers and by a group of former members of the World of Art which had discontinued its activities at that time. The greater part of the Union of Russian Artists remained true to the principles of realism in their work, others were Impressionists and some showed modernist tendencies.... In 1910 the adherents of the World of Art, headed by Benois, left the Union.'[33]

In 1902 Pasternak completed a pastel in the collection of the Russian State Museum, in Leningrad, which represents a staff meeting at the Moscow School of Painting, Sculpture and Architecture. In the lamplight, so favoured by Pasternak at this time in his pictures, we see a group of painters clustered round a table, listening to an invisible speaker. There is Konstantin Korovin, leaning back from the table, thumbs in waistcoat armholes, Apollinarius Vasnetsov, his hand resting on the back of Valentin Serov's chair, and Serov himself, opposite the speaker, a cigarette jutting out of his mouth, intently recording the scene on a pad in front of him. A little group in the background – which includes Pasternak himself – argue a point and someone bears a tray of drinks into the smoke-hazy room, snug and conspiratorial.

At gatherings like this the Moscow artists were to evolve an exhibiting body that was unique in Russia. The principles established by the group 36 Artists were incorporated into the statutes of the Union. Pasternak in his reminiscences recalls how Mikhail Vrubel, who was to have a seminal influence on Russian art of the new century, in helping to frame the statutes worked for 'a complete absence of a hanging committee. Each participant, whether a member or an invited exhibitor, is his own highest tribunal'. Pasternak explains that 'the main principles which had united members of the 36 Artists . . . and which gave its exhibitions a special interest and strength, was, as is known, the . . . most complete freedom of artistic creativity and self-expression. This was a principle absolutely unknown until then, and quite distinct from the rules extant at the Wanderers and the World of Art . . .'. In attempting to embrace such different talents as Vassily Surikov, a veteran Wanderer, whose pictures resembled those of the great Italian monumental painters, and the revolutionary Vrubel, the Union set itself a difficult ideal, and lived up to it.

The Union flourished until 1923, holding annual shows where new talent could hang its works alongside those by some of the finest painters in Russia. The Union exhibition soon became an important event in the artistic calendar, with ever-growing attendances and substantial sales to public and private collections. Yet this body's activities are today little-remembered in Russia and are totally unappreciated in the West. It was a situation that Pasternak was often to dwell on in old age.

There are several reasons for the widespread ignorance in the West of the

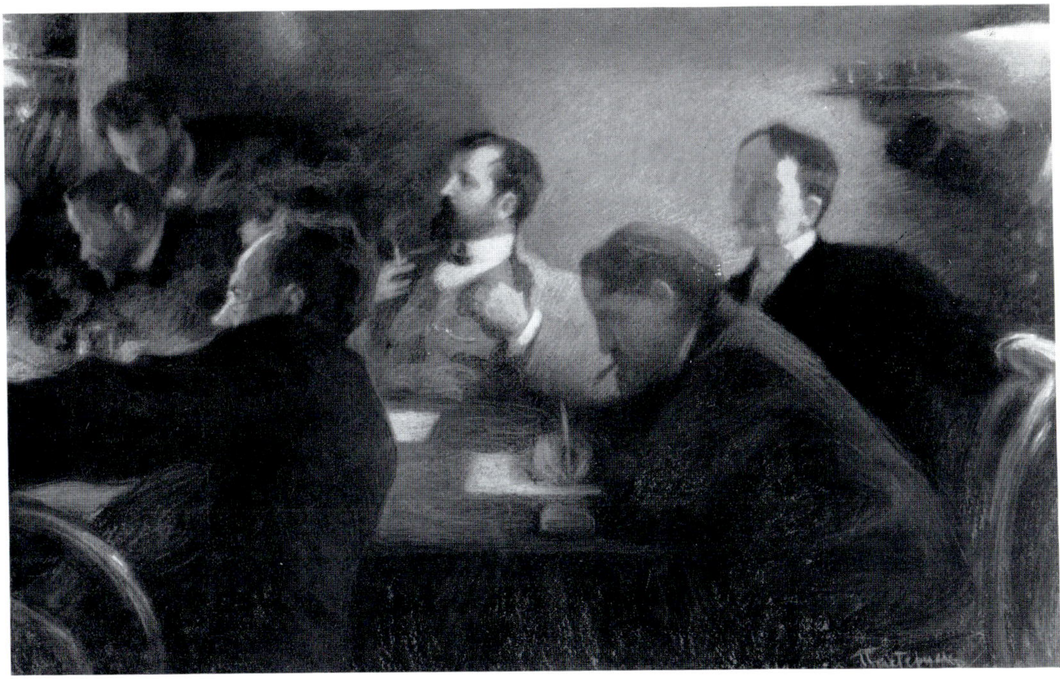

Staff Meeting at the Moscow School of Painting, Sculpture and Architecture, 1902, pastel on paper, 65 × 87 cm. Portrayed are: N. A. Kasatkin, A. E. Arkhipov, the Artist, C. V. Ivanov, K. A. Korovin, V. A. Serov and A. M. Vasnetsov

Union of Russian Artists. On the one hand, there were no journalists and propagandists in their midst, as it was strictly what its name implied: a Union of Russian *Artists*, which had no platform that needed defendants and proselytisers once it was established. They found it abhorrent to indulge in polemics and literary intrigues, and were confident that their work would speak for itself, as indeed it did, at their annual shows. Their adversaries, on the other hand, mostly connected with the St. Petersburg World of Art, had no such scruples. Peculiarly literate publicists and polemicists, they knew how to make themselves heard, how to denigrate those who did not belong to their immediate circle.

Pasternak, writing on the subject at the time, remarks: '*Evidently* it is not enough to be a great artist. It is not enough to form a large and strong community, with a great influence. Obviously this is not enough . . . . The positive aspect of the Union, its silent, deep and serious work in the present-day atmosphere of self-adulation and stark publicity, turns out to be a defect! Yes, *evidently* it is a shortcoming of the Union to have no writers of its own, no critic-tribunes, towncrier-friends, etc., who constantly, on every suitable and unsuitable occasion should proclaim the mission, the merits of the Union, and extol its artists and each other with incessant, importunate, blaring publicity, as done by the World of Art. Whether it is good or bad, press publicity *apparently is a necessity.*'

In his reminiscences Pasternak points out that distortions in the assessment of the development of Russian art in the late nineteenth and early twentieth century – resulting in potted versions of Russian art history: Academy, Wanderers, World of Art, modernist post-war movements – were due to the fact that such history was being written by its very actors. The St. Petersburg painter-historians had absolved themselves from the necessity of an objective approach, so much so that someone at the time referred to Benois' *History of Russian Painting* as a 'History of my Friends'.

The fact that the World of Art movement is now so well remembered and the Union so forgotten does seem largely attributable to the negative influence of those members of the former who joined the Union only to leave in a body in 1910, headed by Alexander Benois. This founding-member of the World of Art, painter and art historian had caused bad feeling by his vicious attacks on the Union whilst still a member. Significantly, the Union of Russian Artists has no place in the two volumes of his *Memoirs*.

Eventually even the veteran, highly revered painter Ilya Repin was goaded into writing public criticism of Benois' attitude to the Union. In a scathing review of an exhibition staged by the *avant-garde* magazine *Apollo*, with which Benois was associated, Repin says: 'The editorial staff of *Apollo* by mistake have taken the name of the god of sun, light, and beauty . . . . It seemed as if all was lost for the eye in this pest-house of the arts . . . . Without taking leave I rushed into the street . . . and thought: "Poor Bakst, he . . . has lost all sense of aesthetic values" . . . . And for him to be guided by the authority of Benois is a sign of hypocrisy, he insults the artist in himself. Alexander Benois, by God's grace – a *dilettante*, who has never seriously learnt to tackle form . . . . All his scenery and pseudo-classical compositions . . . the petty sins of the toiling man.' Repin pays tribute to Benois' illustrations to Pushkin and his work as a bibliographer. 'But as a critic . . . his main purpose is to curry favour with the young, the law-makers of modern art, and to trample on the old . . . . And in his own camp, in the Union, how he has kicked his own comrades, venerable painters – Surikov, Pasternak, Vasnetsov, Vinogradov, and others!!! I don't remember the exact expressions. It hurts me to repeat them. Thus the critic-corporal got hold of the baton in order to raise his own importance and to debase people with a name.'[34]

An interesting comparative estimate of the World of Art and the Union is that of Prince Serge Chsherbatov. In his book *The Painter in Old Russia* he writes of the group with which he was closely associated: 'These Petersburg artists' – that is, the World of Art – 'were cultured, refined and, of course, gifted people, but there were no men of genius among them.'[35] Pointing out the dangers of a decadent aestheticism, Chsherbatov asserts that 'The *Mir Iskusstva* never lived up to the tasks of great painting. On the easy, well-trodden path they had chosen to follow there was a certain point, a certain terminal beyond which they could not penetrate . . . . The road did lead much further, but they lacked the strength, knowledge and skill to pursue it'.[36]

Disturbance at Home – Travel Abroad

The year 1905, which saw Pasternak elevated to the rank of Academician, an established portrait painter and teacher at the Moscow School and an important figure in the youthful Union of Russian Artists, was also to witness an event that rocked an established world to its foundations. The abortive Revolution of 1905 eventually swept its way into the corridors of the Moscow School with serious results that Boris Pasternak so graphically describes. 'By the Director's orders, piles of stones were kept on the landings of the main staircase and lengths of hose connected with the taps for use against possible raiders.

'Every now and then, a crowd marching down our street turned aside and entered the building. Classrooms were occupied, meetings were held in the Assembly Hall, and from the balcony speakers addressed those who had remained in the street below. The College students formed their own militant organisations and our own home guard was on duty at night.' Yet even in this feverish, uncertain atmosphere Leonid Pasternak's pencil was alertly, restlessly recording these historic events.

'Among my father's papers is a drawing of a girl speaking from the balcony; she is wounded and supporting herself against a pillar; dragoons are charging the crowd and shooting at her.'[37] Maxim Gorky, back in Moscow at the end of 1905 at the height of the general strike, invited Pasternak to the editorial offices of various satirical papers he was connected with – such as *The Scourge* and *The Bugaboo*. The two men were to enjoy a close friendship in Moscow which was taken up again the following year in Berlin, where Gorky was in transit to America, his revolutionary activities having prompted the trip.

It was in Berlin that Pasternak did drawings of Gorky, and a portrait etching that found its way into the Gorky Museum, in Moscow. Boris records how one drawing that Pasternak did of Gorky failed to please his friend, the actress Marya Andreyeva. 'Andreyeva disliked it: the cheekbones were too prominent so that the face looked angular,' Boris writes. 'She said: "You haven't understood him. He is Gothic." That was how they spoke in those days.'[38]

The 1905 Revolution eventually made teaching impossible, and while the Moscow School was temporarily closed Pasternak took the opportunity to go with his family to Berlin. It was Boris' first trip abroad. 'Everything was unusual, different from what it was at home. It was less like living than dreaming, or like taking part in some improvisation on the stage, some entertainment without rules, which no one had a duty to take part in or attend. There was nobody you knew, nobody to lay down the law to you.'[39]

The Pasternaks were there for the greater part of 1906 and it proved to be a fruitful visit, in many ways. Leonid was able to meet many painters, such as Max Liebermann and Lovis Corinth – sometimes called German Impressionists, so there was an immediate common interest – Hermann Struck and Heinrich Eickmann. Living in the same house as Eickmann served to reawaken Pasternak's interest in etching, for which he was poorly equipped in Moscow. 'He had handy everything necessary for etching, his own printing press, etc.,' he writes of Eickmann. 'At that time I had the necessary leisure and I could work at his place, experimenting as I liked.' There was also time to complete several portraits.

Pasternak's reputation was now becoming established abroad. His painting *Students Before the Examinations*, that 1895 essay in Impressionism, had helped. After being accepted by the hanging committee of the Wanderers for both their St. Petersburg and Moscow shows, it was withdrawn from their provincial tour. However, it won a gold medal at the Fourth International Exhibition in Munich and was finally acquired by the French government, at the 1900 Paris Universal Exhibition, for the Luxembourg. At the same exhibition, as Tolstoy had forecast, the 33 original watercolours of the *Resurrection* illustrations were put on public display, so that people could judge their true quality. One London publisher, F. Henderson, made a special trip to Paris just to meet the artist and to discuss a Pasternak edition of Tolstoy's works. Pasternak later regretted that he had been so engrossed in other work that he had not pursued the idea. However, he did do further Tolstoy illustrations.

However, other drawings by him were being reproduced in influential magazines such as *The Studio* and *Meister der Farbe*. During the German stay Pasternak also had a successful exhibition at the Galerie Schulte, in Berlin, a shared show which took place in the spring of 1906. An approach was now made by a gallery in Kensington, London. By that time, however, the Pasternaks had to think of returning to Moscow, and after a few weeks' holiday on the Baltic island of Ruegen they left for Russia in the autumn.

One benefit of these European excursions, which now became an important feature of Pasternak's life, was the opportunity of seeing the great pictures there. There had been one trip abroad between the Paris visit of 1900 and the 1906 stay in Berlin. That was in 1904, when a youthful dream of visiting Italy had come true. The amount of money that Pasternak then had at his disposal was limited, and he could do little more than whet his appetite for the art treasures of the country as he scampered around museums, churches and palaces. He had to wait eight years before he could see Italy again, at leisure. In his memoirs Pasternak devotes several pages to his Italian experiences, noting particularly first impressions such as his arrival in Venice, which reminded him of Odessa and childhood. He praises the soft beauty of Giorgione, the colours of Veronese, the depth of Titian and Tintoretto's achievements in his group-paintings.

The second visit to Italy occurred in 1912, when the Pasternaks spent a few weeks on the Mediterranean near Pisa. This journey followed a period in Germany made necessary by Rosa's poor health. The Italian stay gave Pasternak the opportunity to get to know the birthplace of Michelangelo. Tuscany and Umbria, the dreamy small towns, the cloisters, the Florentine picture galleries all made a deep impression on the Russian artist. In his Italian notes Pasternak expresses the great regret that he had often felt when he had been unable to attempt large-scale copies of the masterpieces he saw, as his friend Serov, for example, had copied Velasquez. 'Apart from its usefulness to a young painter, copying an old master must be a great joy, being a kind of conversation, a continuing, intimate contact with him,' Pasternak writes.

To overcome the time problem, Pasternak devised a shorthand method of recording the great works that he saw. 'Not so long ago, without any special formalities, in museums one was allowed to make small copy-sketches (without an easel, and standing). And so I invented a method: a very small box, within it a palette, a piece of canvas, or a little wooden board for a sketch, and other necessary things, and standing, and holding my box as one usually holds a palette, in half an hour or an hour I succeeded in making a coloured, exact sketch of all the tonalities of the original picture. Thus I obtained a very small copy of the given master (not unlike the tonal guidance given in music by the pitch of a tuning fork).

'These quick colouristic sketches then made up what I call my gallery of old masters, and every time I look at them I experience moments of joy, and artistic elation. Everybody calling on me, both fellow-painters and art lovers, used to take delight in and appreciate these sketches, and the original method I used to produce them.' Pasternak lists the sketches he made, which included works by Bennozzo Gozzoli, Andrea Orcagna, Rembrandt, Rubens, Vandyke, Titian, Tintoretto, Velasquez and Veronese, concluding that Gozzoli's *Grape-Gatherers* and Orcagna's *Triumph of Death* from frescoes in Campo Santo, Pisa, were the most successful, from the point of view of colour and because of their monumental design. As during the Second World War the greater part of the frescoes was destroyed, Pasternak's studies are of considerable historical value.

Between these two Italian trips and following the 1906 stay in Berlin, the Pasternaks were to travel elsewhere in Europe during the first decade of this century. In 1907 they visited Holland, Belgium and – unexpectedly – England. They were in Bruges for the four-hundredth anniversary of *Les Fastes de la Toison d'Or*, where there was a large exhibition of 800 works of art, including 270 pictures.

The Pasternaks in Holland and Belgium sated themselves with the works of the Flemish masters. Frans Hals and Rembrandt were Leonid's favourites, especially Rembrandt. 'It is recognized that while looking at a work of art we artists mainly consider aspects such as form, colour and technique. But looking at Rembrandt, all this recedes into the background – so moving, so human and profound are his creations. The more I looked at Rembrandt, the more my conviction grew that, although of course he belongs to the whole world, he must be nearest (apart from his own, Dutch, kinsmen) to the Jewish people,' Pasternak, himself of Jewish ancestry, writes. 'Although before and after him artists represented the Bible and Jewish life, Rembrandt alone, this man of genius and this non-Jew, succeeded in penetrating so deeply into the biblical subject-matter, and with such warmth and affection, representing the real Jewish essence.

'Was it an inner kinship between the sufferer-people and the sufferer-artist? Difficult to say. It is known, however, that Rembrandt never parted with the Bible. Further, that he came to live in the poor Jewish quarter of Amsterdam. Also that in old age Rembrandt was poor, sick and lonely. That his friends then were the Jewish doctor, the famous, learned Manasse,* whom Rembrandt portrayed, as he did other rabbis. And, beyond doubt, in those narrow, dirty little streets he encountered his kings – his Saul and his Davids; doubtless, too, the Jewish poor in rags, the beggars of this district, its artisans and synagogue attendants became the models for his magnificent biblical compositions.' It is not surprising that Pasternak took the trouble to publish in the 1920's in Berlin a small monograph on Rembrandt and the Jewish ethos, illustrated with some of that painter's greatest pictures.†

When they were in England during the same 1907 trip the Pasternaks were as enthusiastic about acquainting themselves with the English school as they had been about the Continental ones. During this first visit to England Pasternak was especially impressed by the late-eighteenth-century portraitists, of whose pictures he had only seen reproductions in Moscow. Seeing the originals of Gainsborough, Romney, Lawrence and, above all, Reynolds, 'the most perfect *virtuoso* and the greatest master of them all', was a long-felt wish fulfilled. Pasternak admired the manner in which they had in their different ways represented 'the century's main characteristics – the decorativeness, the impressive appearance of a grand style'. Later on in life he was to develop considerable respect for some of the Scottish painters, such as Raeburn, having seen a large exhibition of this school, although his admiration for the late-eighteenth-century English portraitists became modified. However, although during another London trip their pictures 'appeared to me less interesting with their empty showiness', he conceded that 'the artists themselves are masters of form, and each one of them "sits firmly in the saddle", their portraits being calculated mainly to produce a decorative effect'.

Two English painters' works which surprised Pasternak when he first visited London, for whom he retained untarnished regard, were Constable and, more especially, Turner. 'We, on the Continent, are unable to form an opinion of him,' he writes. 'In a way he was a revelation to me, as I am of the opinion that he has influenced the French Impressionists, or rather, that he was the first to have started off light painting and what is known by the term *plein air*. The temperament of this visionary, this seeker of new ways in painting, and his strivings are best shown in one of his studies which does not hang in the Tate any more, at least unfortunately I could not locate it in the vast Turner collection in the gallery.

* Rabbi Manasseh Ben Israel
† *Rembrandt and Judaism*. By Leonid Pasternak, S. D. Zal'tsman (Berlin 1923), in Russian.

54

I was overwhelmed by the unexpectedness of an inscription on the picture, an inscription which sounded like an imperious motto of his: "*Fiat lux, fiat color*" .... Like all landscape painters of his time he had started with darkish pictures, in imitation of the Dutch brown landscapes – yet he finished with visions, dreams, fantasies in painting (an English tendency), yet I have to acknowledge Turner's immense influence on French art.'

Pasternak sketched in London's galleries as he had on the Continent, yet even his deft draughtsmanship was unequal to one task – the Elgin Marbles in the British Museum. His wife waited patiently while he worked, but eventually he had to give up. He told the story to Serov later in Moscow. With a typical gesture his friend replied: '*I* couldn't do them *either*!'

A Visit to Esher
The trip to England was an unplanned part of the Pasternaks' 1907 European itinerary. It had its beginnings in a series of letters which Leonid had received in Moscow the previous year from a Mr. Vincent, of London. Vincent had seen the artist's drawings of children reproduced in *The Studio* and admired them so much that he invited Pasternak to London to paint his eight-year-old daughter. The artist was greatly impressed by this invitation from another country, especially one where there was a tradition of good portrait-painting. The Pasternaks had long intended to see England. Rosa, however, was of a nervous disposition, and – as Leonid points out in his reminiscences – 'only the fear of crossing the "eternally stormy channel" let us postpone the undertaking. I answered Mr. V. that I might come next summer; we planned to go to Holland and Belgium, anyway; perhaps we would pluck up courage to cross over to England, too'.

The article that had tempted Vincent to write to Pasternak was one by Pavel Ettinger, which covered several pages of *The Studio* and which was well illustrated with masterly line and line-and-wash drawings: child and mother-and-child studies. Pasternak was never an artist to court the critics, being too self-effacing to publicise his own work. His relationship with Ettinger was another matter, however. Ettinger was a bank clerk, and noted part-time writer on art. He was also a close friend of the painter's, and they continued to maintain contact by letter when later Pasternak left Moscow. Ettinger's *Studio* article on Pasternak's draughtsmanship is thus valuable, because he was in the position of having seen his subject's skills develop over a period. That he is an objective critic, however, is indicated by his statement that: 'Apart from the group of young St. Petersburg artists ... which attached itself to the journal *Mir Isskoustva* [*World of Art*], and worked mainly in the decorative style, the number of good draughtsmen and illustrators in Russia is exceedingly small, especially so far as the older generation is concerned.' He adds: 'Among these latter Leonid Pasternak occupies a quite exceptional place.'[40]

Ettinger judges Pasternak 'a painter of the first rank', citing *Students Before*

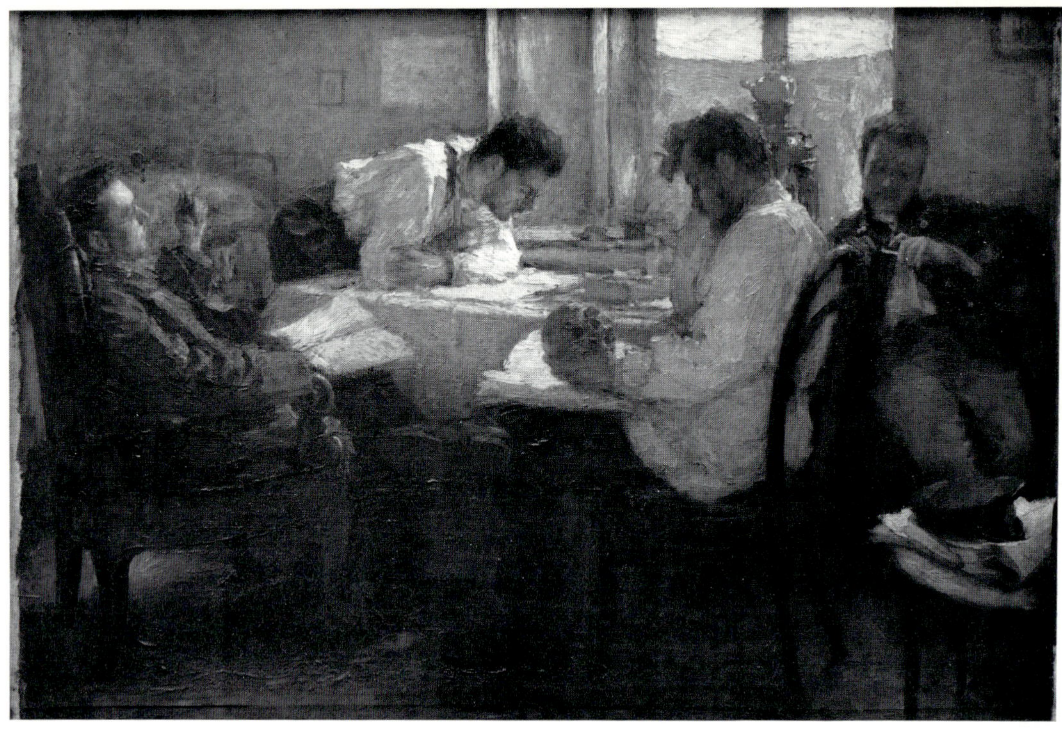

Students Before the Examinations, 1895, oil on canvas, 385 × 551 cm.

the Examinations and *Tolstoy with his Family*, yet considers his drawings perhaps the most important feature of his output. 'Of all the various techniques employed by the draughtsman scarcely one there is which this artist has not brought into use. At first he seems to have chiefly employed Chinese-black, charcoal, and ink, and rarely water-colour; but of recent years he has displayed a preference for coloured chalks and pastel in proportion to the increasingly prominent *rôle* assumed by the element of colour in his works. His pen-and-ink drawings, formerly so abundant, have latterly become fewer and fewer: the note of colour has grown stronger and stronger; and so far as his very latest period is concerned, coloured drawings are invariably the rule . . . . The high artistic merit of drawings such as these is generally realised to the full . . . in the collector's portfolio; for there alone can they display completely their innate sympathy and warmth of treatment.'

Ettinger indicates that everyday family life – the responsibilities of which had caused Pasternak such anxiety immediately prior to his marriage – had provided the artist with a theme for some of his finest drawings and oil studies. 'With his fine gift of observation he watches the children at work and play, the mother nursing her baby, or the little daughter prettily nestling by her side, or some cosy bath scene in the nursery, or some other similar every-day subject, and notes it

56

rapidly on paper or cardboard. Naturally he is here in danger of recording that which is trifling or insignificant; yet so sure is his handling of each characteristic pose and movement, so brilliant his technique, so aesthetic his feeling, that the artist always contrives to succeed . . . . The sure, solid taste of the artist never fails to tell him where to draw the line between sentiment and sentimentality.'

Anxious about the Channel crossing and apprehensive about living up to Ettinger's panegyric, Pasternak and his wife – having exhausted the museums and art galleries – pottered around Bruges and Ostend. There they sat on the beach and looked longingly in the direction of England. It was during one of the open-air *Toison d'Or* celebrations that Pasternak ran into his old Berlin friend, the painter Hermann Struck. 'He had just returned from London – weather and crossing had been excellent. When he heard about our "sittings" in Ostend, on the beach, and of our unforgiveable indecisiveness, he began to talk us into going, and insisted that right now, without reflecting, we should go to Ostend, take a ticket and in the evening go to London. "The weather," he said, "is exceptionally calm, and you will see that without noticing it, you will be in Dover. I'll come with you to Ostend, I will take the tickets . . . or, else, I know, you will not leave." '

After repeated anxious inquiries of the porters about the weather prospects, concern about the rocking of the boat when they first stepped on it and a glass of brandy in the buffet to steady nerves, the Pasternaks almost enjoyed the sea-trip, even dozed off. 'And opening our eyes we saw that we were near the white coast of England! Dover!! And then after about two hours we were in London, on a London station. Curious carriages – "cabs" – peculiar, like the peculiar people there. All was peculiar, original . . . .'

Another adventure was ahead. After a bout of gallery- and museum-visiting, and having drawn Vincent's little girl, the Pasternaks received an invitation from their host's brother and sister to visit them at their Esher, Surrey, country house. 'Much as we were flattered . . . we had to decline the invitation, simply because on our journey we had no suitable "visiting" clothes. When travelling abroad without the intention of visiting anybody, I preferred to travel "lightly" without burdensome trunks, or innumerable suitcases . . . to avoid possible customs complications. However firmly we refused to go, explaining quite candidly that this was only a question of proper appearance, he would not take no for an answer, and said that our fears were unfounded.' They left the following Sunday in Vincent's car.

The Pasternaks' apprehension turned to alarm when they realised that the country house was Esher Place, once the residence of Cardinal Wolsey, although in 1907 it was much changed. 'The residential part of the estate was a building in a Louis XVI style,' writes Pasternak. 'One had to ascend to it gradually, it was situated among flower gardens, clipped hedges, peacock-shaped shrubs, and so on. This "introduction" alone, to the main entrance, showed us that we, with our travelling suits . . . had come to the wrong place! . . . Of course, the butler who opened the door was better dressed than myself – he wore not black as I had expected, but a kind of light-grey tails . . . .

'The butler asked us to inscribe our names in the book of "prominent visitors" . . . . The English are fond of ranks and titles, and the rank of an Academician is well appreciated. As I had this title, and also in order to make up for our informal appearance, I entered it in the book, which obviously pleased the butler, and slightly relieved me in my embarrassment . . . . Then he asked us upstairs where another servant already waited with jugs of cold and warm water for "ablutions".

'We then descended into the main reception hall where we were greeted by the host advancing in our direction. He wore a Scottish kilt, he was tall, handsome, cheerful, with an open, serene countenance. His whole figure exhaled health, carefree peacefulness, the absence of our Russian life-"problems" and difficulties – you could feel an inner strength, and a tranquil confidence in himself and his surroundings. He introduced us to his wife – tall, slender, middle-aged but looking young, apparently a former beauty and society "lioness", of a very aristocratic family, well known in the world of sport, very lively and witty. First of all we said how sorry we were for our appearance . . . . The English are fond of the original, perhaps they took it as a desire on our part to be original – perhaps . . . .'

By the time that the Pasternaks met him Edgar Vincent, the subject of Leonid's comments, had had a chequered career that was to diversify and was to gain distinction with the passing years. In 1907 he was 50, and had behind him long service in the army, banking and financial administration in the Near East. Tall and imposing, as Pasternak describes him, he had an agile, questioning mind and powers of speech that were to take him into politics and ultimately were to make him a valuable recruit to the British diplomatic service. He had bought Esher Place in 1897. Described by Nikolaus Pevsner as 'a very large Frenchy mansion',[41] it was the result of development going back to the fifteenth century.

The Pasternaks' new host led them through his picture collection, which included a Rembrandt, a good Frans Hals and three portraits of their hostess, by Benjamin Constant, Franz von Lenbach and John Singer Sargent. When Edgar Vincent had married Helen Venetia Duncombe, daughter of the first Earl of Feversham, of Ryedale, in 1890, she was one of the reigning beauties of London, and was a popular subject with portrait painters. Pasternak preferred the Sargent to the Lenbach and Constant portraits of her.

'Lunch brought further surprises,' he writes. 'First, the beautiful table of black polished wood at which we four were seated (the brother had already left) had no tablecloth, whereas another one, much smaller, was covered by a white tablecloth; secondly, the little niece with her governess sat at this separate table.'

After lunch it emerged that their host was musical, and Rosa Pasternak was asked to play a few pieces on the piano. 'Her unusual, artistic, unique musical interpretation made the music-lover ask her for more, and more – without end,' Pasternak recalls. It was a painful performance, for Rosa was suffering from an abscess under the arm which called for minor surgical treatment when they returned to their hotel, prompted an earlier departure from England than had been planned, and then necessitated further surgery in Moscow.

There were other novelties for the Russian guests, which Pasternak records with fascination. 'The afternoon tea was served very interestingly in the garden. An enormous red carpet was spread over the famous English silky lawn under a huge, very old and very tall tree, whose branches were supported by iron brackets, and whose trunk could only be encircled by the arms of several people. This deep red against a background of luscious greenness made a strikingly solemn impression.' Pasternak was also fascinated by the host's or hostess' nephews, two boys who arrived with a young man shortly after lunch. He remarks in his reminiscences how only the elder of the boys had a title, the other 'was not titled at all, an ordinary mortal . . . '.

With these visitors the Pasternaks left by train for London that evening. But before they left, 'my hospitable host tried to talk me into moving to England for good where, according to him, I would be "up to my neck" in work (portrait commissions, etc.), and where I would "roll in gold" – but I was so fond of Moscow, my activities in the School and all that was dear to me there that, of course, I could not even consider following his advice . . . '.

Thus, in a throwaway manner, Pasternak dismisses his host's suggestion that he work in England. Yet if acted upon it would have changed his life completely. Freed from his pedagogic duties and brought into the mainstream of European painting whilst at the height of his powers as an artist, such a move would almost certainly have ensured a brilliant future for Pasternak.

'Come to us. You will not regret it,' his Esher host had commented, and the facts give weight to this confident prediction. In 1914 Edgar Vincent was raised to the peerage as Baron D'Abernon of Esher, in 1917 was promoted G.C.M.G., then in 1920 Lloyd George selected him to be the first ambassador to the new German republic. He remained in Berlin until 1926 and his success was such that in that year he was advanced to a viscountcy and appointed G.C.B. His extensive public duties, many related to the arts – he was a trustee of both the National and Tate Galleries – brought him into contact with all the leading men of his day. With such a sponsor, Pasternak would have been assured of a portrait-painting connection second to none. D'Abernon himself was painted by Ambrose McEvoy and Augustus John. John's full-length portrayal of the Viscount in his robes, one of only two ceremonial pictures by him, is now in the Tate Gallery's collection.

The Russian painter and the English diplomat were to meet once more, in very different circumstances. During a visit to Berlin in 1921 Pasternak was told that the Edgar Vincent on whom he had called at Esher was now Baron D'Abernon, British ambassador. Coincidentally, this happened at the house of Hermann

Struck, the painter friend who had in Belgium goaded the Pasternaks into visiting England. Pasternak was doubtful that Vincent really was D'Abernon. 'Naturally, next day I checked the truth of this statement,' he writes, 'and was very cordially welcomed by Lord D'Abernon.'

Esher Place today is structurally much the same as when Pasternak visited it. Lord D'Abernon sold it in 1936, five years before he died, when it became a girls' school. The Electrical, Electronic Telecommunication and Plumbing Union, which now occupies the building, then took it over as a training college in 1952. The Benjamin Constant portrait of Lady D'Abernon which Pasternak commented on is still at Esher Place, let into a wall.

Moscow – the Final Years
The Moscow to which the Pasternaks returned after their European journeyings in 1907 was a city bubbling with artistic activity. The intellectual climate during the decade up to the Revolution of 1917 was a bracing one for young painters and writers.

Boris Pasternak captures the flavour well in *An Essay in Autobiography*. 'It was from about 1907 that a crop of new publishers started springing up like mushrooms, modern compositions were performed at many concerts, and art exhibitions opened one after another – "The World of Art", "The Golden Fleece", "The Knave of Diamonds", "The Donkey's Tail", "The Blue Rose". Among the many Russian names – Somov, Sapunov, Sudeykin, Krymov, Laryonov, Goncharova – flickered the names of Frenchmen – Bonnard, Vuillard. Pictures by Matisse and sculptures by Rodin arrived from Paris and could be seen at The Golden Fleece, in darkly curtained halls which smelled of mould like hot-houses, so crowded were they with pots of hyacinths.'[42]

Once the Union was established, in 1903, many of the Petersburg World of Art members became involved in the Moscow shows. In the December 1906 exhibition of the Union quite a few of the pictures had been seen previously at World of Art shows, notably those by Symbolist painters. These were mostly students of the Moscow School, who emerged as the Blue Rose group cited by Boris Pasternak after the 1906 show.

Thus it was students of Levitan, Serov and Pasternak and the Moscow School who spearheaded the numerous splinter-groups which proliferated up to the Revolution. A series of exhibitions organized by the Blue Rose and its magazine *Golden Fleece* in 1907–8–9 at first featured strongly the French Post-Impressionists and pre-Cubist painters. Eventually, however, there was a reaction against the French influence, after which the Primitivism and what has been termed Cubo-Futurism of Larionov and Goncharova gained sway, blazing the way for Kasimir Malevich, Vladimir Tatlin and Constructivism and Suprematism. Larionov and Goncharova were both Moscow School students while Pasternak was there. It says much for the open-mindedness of the Union of Russian Artists which he and other Moscow School teachers had helped to found that Tatlin, another Moscow student, was admitted as a fellow-exhibitor.

Pasternak did not approve of the new artistic tendencies, 'so unbalanced, so fickle, when new movements explode like fireworks and perish as quickly; when annual new outlooks and tastes hired from abroad, like fashionable hats, live one season only'. To him, 'all these changing "isms" (such as Futurism, Cubism, Suprematism, Aformism, Purism, Dadaism, etc.), in their decadence became a serious threat, not so much to art as to *artistic education*: they undermined the fundamentals of elementary artistic tuition, and this for a long time', he reminisces in old age. 'These "temporary epidemics" infected all art schools, in the West as well as in our country, and even now the damage they caused makes itself felt in the *lack of adequate artistic education*. Our School suffered most . . . .

'V. A. Serov, who found teaching burdensome and intended to leave the School anyway, very early guessed the real danger of these "isms",' writes Pasternak. When Serov decided to leave, Pasternak urged him to stay and use his good influence in the School. 'What! – *I* should stay and teach these Larionovs?!' was Serov's retort, referring to the student who, Camilla Gray recounts, eventually was expelled from the School after the director, Prince Lvov, had asked him to remove some of his works from the monthly inspection exhibition. Larionov, who had taken up the entire space alloted to students of his year, refused to do so. Boris Pasternak comments on this period: 'Modesty, gratitude, sense of truth, were not in currency among the young artistic circles of the left; such feelings were considered mawkish. The proper thing was to be insolent and strut about sticking one's nose up in the air'.[43]

Those teachers at the School – such as Pasternak and Serov – who disagreed with the revolutionary trends in painting just mentioned could today too easily be dismissed as traditional diehards, but this would be an unjust assessment. For the men who felt a very real unease about the new, disruptive influences themselves had reputations as iconoclasts that were still fresh. The Union which they had formed only a few years before had itself challenged the orthodoxy of the Wanderers. Both Pasternak and Serov had during the 1905 Revolution drawn cartoons for the satirical and revolutionary press. Serov had actually resigned from the Academy when his protest at the Massacre of the Ninth of January was rejected.

In spite of the disruptive influence of the new trends, the School succeeded in carrying on with its work. Excited by developments he had seen in graphic reproduction techniques in the West, Pasternak strove to pass on this knowledge to younger artists, and himself took part in good-quality, illustrated popular publication ventures. He was dissatisfied with the cheap and tasteless oleographs that were sold to the poor, and believed that old and new painters' works should be made available to those 'who cannot indulge in the luxury of buying expensive pictures'. For Pasternak, 'new horizons opened, new possibilities of making

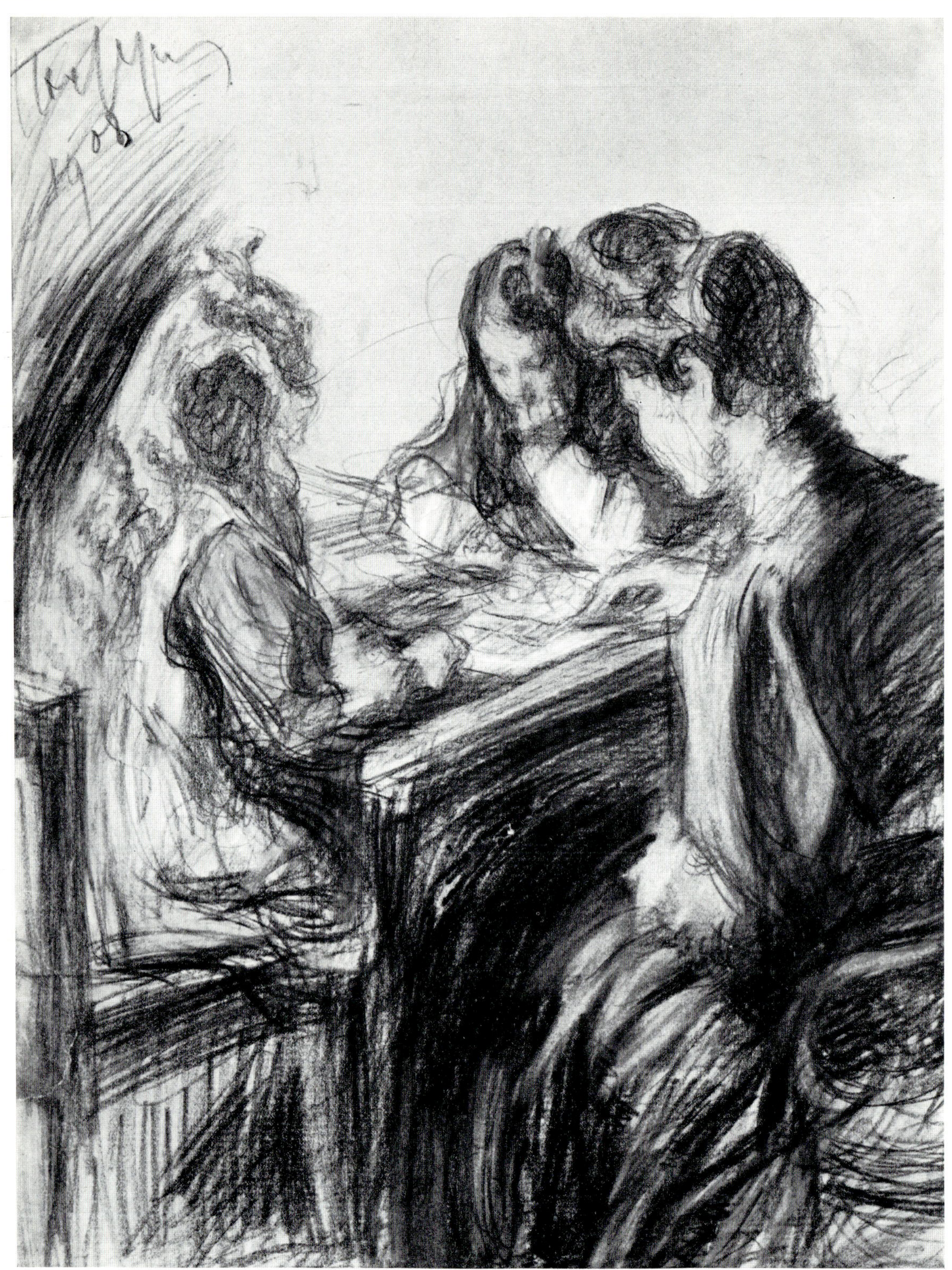

Josephine and Lydia with their German Governess, 1908, charcoal and red chalk, 35·5 × 28 cm.

accessible to the people highly artistic creations both in reproduction, and as independent, original work'. In addition to new ways with monochrome there was 'especially coloured auto-lithography. This is a procedure in which the artist *himself* draws on the lithographic stone (or on paper, from which the image is *then* transferred to the stone). Thus the intervention of a lithographic worker and his possible mistakes are eliminated'.

Particularly successful was Pasternak's lithograph *Tolstoy at Work*, of 1908, which penetrated to all parts of Russia. Although technically of a high standard, it was moderately priced so that those of modest means could afford it.

The years 1910 and 1911 brought tragic losses for Pasternak, when first Tolstoy and then Serov died. Boris Pasternak recollects that when he arrived home late one night, in November 1910, he found that his father had been summoned by telegram to Astapovo, the now famous little railway station, where Tolstoy, on his flight from Yasnaya Polyana, had died of pneumonia at the stationmaster's house. Pasternak was to make a last drawing of Tolstoy, at the request of Sofya Andreyevna, Tolstoy's widow. Boris – then a student at Moscow University – left for Astapovo with his father. In *An Essay in Autobiography* he gives a powerful account of the long journey, their reception by the distraught Countess who had followed her husband there, his own feelings and thoughts about it, and the whole atmosphere of the room where Tolstoy lay dead.

The Count lay in a peasant's blouse, on a simple iron bed. 'The place bristled with fir saplings which stood round the bed, their outlines sharpened by the setting sun. Four slanting sheaves of light reached across the room and threw over the corner where the body lay the sign of the big shadow of the crosspiece of the window and the small, childish crosses of the shadows of the firs.'[44] Boris watched while his father worked, the result of which was a large drawing in coloured chalks of Tolstoy surrounded by the small fir trees. The picture now hangs in the Tolstoy Museum, in Moscow.

In November 1911, at Tolstoy's memorial concert in the Moscow Conservatoire, Rosa Pasternak appeared in public for the last time. Once again she played the piano part in Chaikovsky's A-minor trio, which she had first played to Tolstoy 18 years before.

By 1912 Rosa's heart attacks, increasing in number and strength, made it imperative to undertake the already-mentioned journey abroad. The treatment at Bad Kissingen, in Bavaria, was followed by several weeks by the sea, near Pisa. The strenuous treatment at the German spa temporarily alleviated Rosa's trouble and the Pasternaks planned a return, but the outbreak of the First World War made this impossible. Leonid now did all he could to encourage and help his wife, and would sit for hours at her bedside when her spirits were at their lowest.

Soon after the beginning of the First World War Pasternak was approached by a delegation from the city of Moscow which requested that he draw a poster to

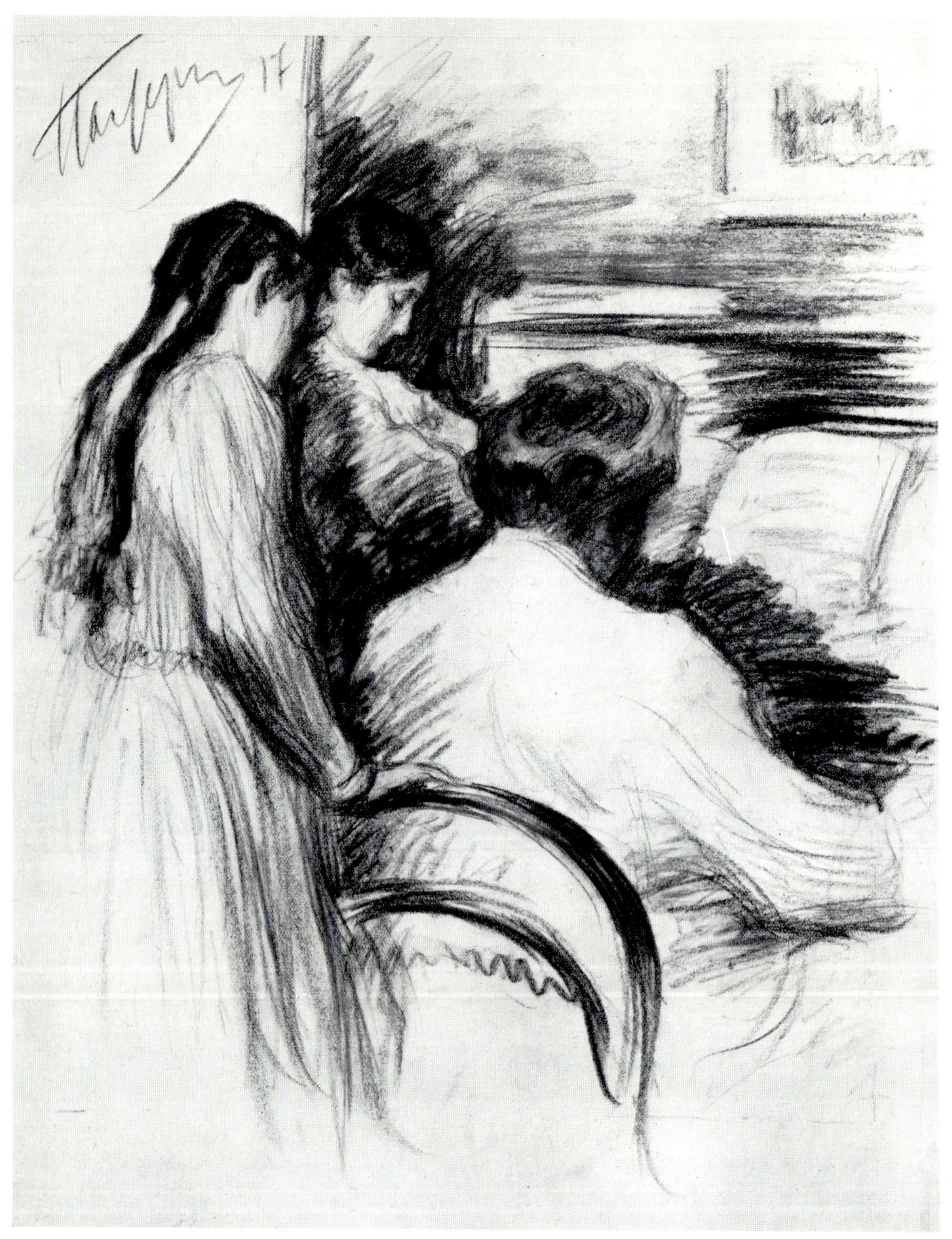

Rosa at the Piano, with her Daughters, 1917, charcoal, 32·5 × 25·5 cm.

advertise a collection in aid of war victims. 'I asked them to send me a soldier in full battledress, so that I could draw from life, and then from my sketch make an auto-lithograph, that is, myself draw on the lithographic stone. Thus each copy would be an *original*. If I am not mistaken, I was the first in Russia to produce such a poster by the method of auto-lithography. My poster, produced in a few colours on the biggest lithographic stone, represented a wounded soldier leaning against a wall.

'I was amazed by its success and popularity, when my poster was stuck up all over Moscow on the day of the collection. Crowds gathered in front of it and would not move. Village women cried . . . . Famous artists were in charge of the collection. They sold picture postcards of my soldier, too, hundreds of thousands of copies. I transferred the unrestricted right of reproduction and of use to the city of Moscow. The material success of this venture, both in Moscow and in other Russian cities, also exceeded all the expectations of the organizers of this charitable collection. From Petersburg, the State Duma President Rodzianko asked me to let him have about a hundred thousand copies for his collection of donations, and so on. The best English art magazine, *Studio* (interested in pure graphic art, too), reproduced my soldier.'*

It was through an adjutant from St. Petersburg, who had come to ask Pasternak to draw a cover for a military hospital periodical which had royal support, that the artist learned of Nicholas II's dissatisfaction with *The Wounded Soldier*. Instead of evoking bravery and courage, complained the Emperor, it only called forth compassion.

The Revolution of 1917 brought a cry for popular art, and Leonid – with his urge to take good pictures to everyone – was caught up in events. In about 1918, he recalls, 'I came for a day to Moscow from the country where I was staying. I was surprised to see my poster *The Wounded Soldier* reprinted and stuck all over Moscow again. This was done without my knowledge, and was meant as anti-war propaganda. The chairman of the State Publishing House, a very nice man, explained to me that everything printed by them belonged to them, and that no special permission was required. He also asked me to give them "something else". Accordingly I drew for them a few portraits, and group-pictures – meetings, conferences, and so on (later acquired by the Soviet government for the Lenin Museum, Tretyakov Gallery, etc.)'.

Among Pasternak's many pictures of famous men, those of Lenin are among the most successful, and they are still being discovered. Writing in *Isvestia* in 1965, S. Burdiansky told of 'a completely unknown pencil portrait of Vladimir Il'itch Lenin, made from life in 1920. Among the very few drawings of Vladimir Il'itch from life known to us, the portrait drawings by the painter Academician

The Studio, February 1915, page 63. Having pointed out that Russian art during the war had been confined mainly to producing popular coloured prints, the magazine published *The Wounded Soldier* and a drawing by Sergei Vinogradov as 'evidence of the activity of artists of a higher calibre'.

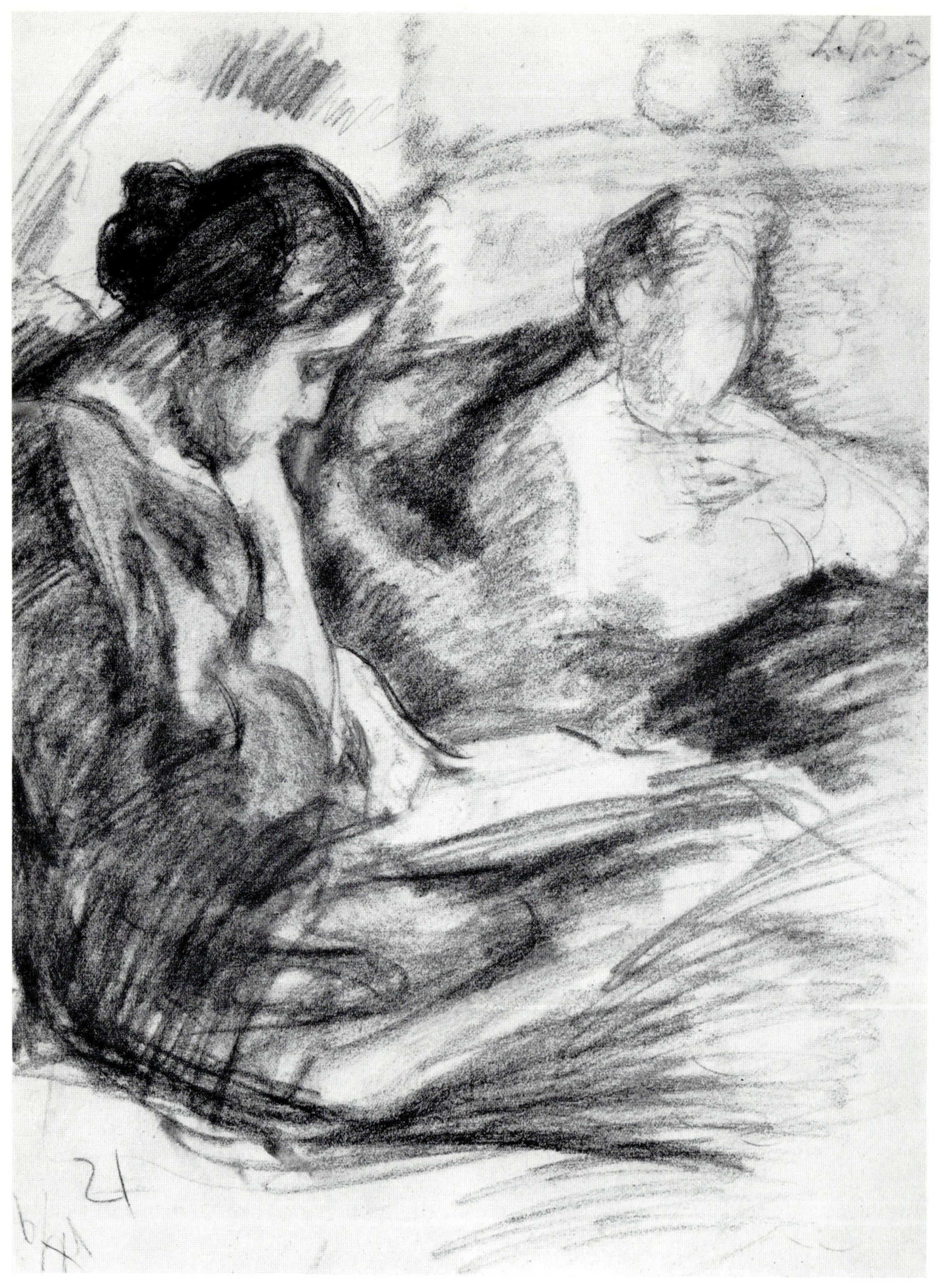

The Artist's Wife and Josephine Reading, 1921, charcoal, 33 × 25·5 cm.

L. O. Pasternak occupy a special place . . . . In my hands now I have the artist's notebook with perforated detachable pages . . . . Forty-five years have elapsed since the chairman of the V.C.I.K.,* M. I. Kalinin, signed the documents enabling the artist to immortalise Lenin . . . . To this day reminders of that occasion exist: an official permit to work in the Kremlin, with a photo, certificates on the blanks of the V.C.I.K. and the Komintern . . . .

'The artist made a series of interesting sketches in those days, at the meetings of the Soviets, the sessions of the V.C.I.K., and congresses of the Komintern; in the Bol'shoi Theatre, for a big composition, he made a watercolour study, during the conference of the VII All-Russian Meeting of the Soviets in Moscow. Many years later he worked on the creation of a colour portrait of Lenin, but unfortunately he could not finish the composition . . . . And on a separate page I find what I have been looking for: this sketch from life . . . . Intense, vivid thought illumines Vladimir Il'itch's features – with astonishing truthfulness the expression has been captured of will, concentration and of a profound intelligence'.[45]

Just before and during the First World War, the disruptive activities of extreme groups, both outside and inside the Moscow School, made teaching there more and more difficult and frustrating. Pasternak, in his reminiscences, recalls how the staff of the School had to fight to maintain the most elementary truths of artistic tuition. 'Less and less energy and enthusiasm could I muster, too. On the contrary, my conviction grew that no attempt to help the School would meet with success . . . . I wanted to leave, but my resignation would not be accepted.'

After the Revolution the Pasternaks hoped again to travel to Germany, so that Rosa's treatment might at last be resumed. The insecurity of the immediate post-war years, with the disruption of transport, the terrible typhus epidemic, the unprecedented inflation, the lack of essential foodstuffs and fuel and all the other privations made daily life a continuous struggle for survival. It was especially taxing for older people. The exasperating difficulties of art teaching in this period of turmoil additionally sapped the health of Leonid, too. Despite protests he now handed in his resignation.

'I felt sorry, though, to leave four or five of my pupils, gifted and of very varied abilities, who still had to complete their art education.' As a compromise he agreed to teach a small group privately, 'for I was convinced that they would develop into very interesting artists, original, unlike one another. This – as I learned later – some of them did indeed.†

'Time went on, and I began preparations for going abroad with my wife, who had to undergo treatment in Germany.' This was in 1921, when restrictions on foreign travel began to be relaxed. Josephine, the elder daughter, applied for and

---

* V.C.I.K.: All-Russian Central Executive Committee

† It has not been possible to establish who these artists were.

got permission to go abroad, and left Moscow in June. 'On the eve of my departure a kind of deputation called on me, representing those thirsting to continue their education, both men and women, with a request to "reconstruct" the School. I pointed to my luggage, to my sick wife, to my departure in a few days' time, and said that I was genuinely sad not to be able to help them.' Thus in the autumn of 1921 Leonid and Rosa Pasternak, accompanied by their younger daughter, left for Berlin.

Berlin and Successful Exhibitions

The first years in Berlin meant a physical and artistic rebirth for the Pasternaks. The medical treatment peculiar to Germany at that time, which her doctor had recommended in Moscow, slowly but effectively overcame Rosa's heart trouble. The relief from worry about his wife's health, release from the many difficulties in Moscow and the comparative ease and freedom of life in the German capital – in spite of economic troubles following Germany's recent defeat – liberated Leonid to work with a new zest. He praises in his memoirs the openness of people there towards artistic experiment, the generosity of a creative colony which welcomed a foreigner into its midst, and the toleration and impartiality of the press.

It has already been mentioned that Rosa's musical connection had introduced Pasternak to a new range of subjects. Germany meant an extension of his interests. 'I became acquainted with the Berlin society which cultivated, and was genuinely fond of, painting, music, drama – any art. . . . From the first days of my temporary stay in Berlin I began to work intensively,' he writes, 'painting mainly portraits – eagerly, freely, boldly, not trying to please the public, or the critics, or the press.' He also engaged in auto-lithography, etching and other graphic work (portraits of Cohen, Struck, Karpov, Verhaeren, Beethoven, and so on). Pasternak now added to his reputation for portraits of women by completing several striking examples in this *genre*. A number are reproduced in Max Osborn's monograph on him.

Suritz, the Soviet ambassador, often invited the Pasternaks to receptions at the Embassy, where they met many interesting people, including the diplomats of other countries. This enabled Leonid to sketch, for example, Suritz's wife and daughters, and the Russian composer Prokofiev at the piano. Catching the essential quality of a person was Pasternak's special gift as a portraitist. Thus, in 1962, when many members of the Russian colony attended the Pasternak centenary exhibition in Munich, there were those who stopped and caught their breath before certain likenesses, murmuring: 'Ah, that is how *I* knew him, too.' Notable figures in the world of science (Einstein, von Harnack), art (Lovis Corinth, Max Liebermann), music (Mischa Elman, Eisner) and literature (Gerhard Hauptmann, Rilke) were among Pasternak's sitters.

The friendship between Pasternak and the German poet Rainer Maria Rilke, whom he had sketched earlier, extended back over many years. There had been an occasion when Pasternak had helped Rilke and some friends to locate Tolstoy, as it was an ambition of the poet's to meet him. There are several versions of the encounter. Leonid mentions it in an autobiographical fragment that was published in the early 1930's; Boris – who was as a young man greatly impressed by Rilke's work – gives a time-muddled account of it in *An Essay in Autobiography*; but Rilke himself, writing excitedly to a friend very shortly after the visit, in May 1900, graphically tells of meeting Pasternak, and of the resulting visit to Tolstoy. In March 1926 Rilke, writing to Pasternak in Germany, speaks warmly of their long friendship and Boris' growing reputation, adding: 'To know you living and working in comparatively normal circumstances, surrounded by a part of your family, is a good happy knowledge to me! And prejudiced though I am against having my portrait made, if proximity in space permits and we see each other again, I shall be proud to occupy a modest place in the ranks of your models.'[46]

Pasternak soon began to find outlets for his German work. 'Having received an invitation from the "Secession" to give them something *hors concours* (that is, being exempt from the judgement of the hanging committee), I gave them my oil portrait of Einstein,' he writes, 'then, after a year or two, some still life watercolours.' Josephine Pasternak recalls that when the Einstein portrait was being painted her mother was unable to go into the studio to talk with the sitter, so she herself went. Then a young woman interested in philosophy, she tentatively brought up the subject, which managed to animate Einstein as Pasternak liked. When the sitting was over Einstein remarked that their conversation had, in a Pavlovian way, 'whetted my appetite again to do something philosophical'.

In the late 1920's, encouraged by friends and relations, Pasternak 'came to the conclusion that I had to arrange my own exhibition, where the public could get acquainted with different aspects of my work'. Pasternak's new period of creativity had resulted in a variety of projects: his work was shown in Holland; German periodicals were publishing his pictures, such as the Einstein portrait, and his drawing of Chaliapin, done whilst the singer was rehearsing for a recital in Berlin; his lithograph of Beethoven was completed to commemorate the centenary of the composer's death; Pasternak was painting his portraits of the painter Lovis Corinth, the theologian Adolf von Harnack, and of Tolstoy, at the centenary of his birth, for an exhibition in Russia. These examples indicate the prodigious industry and breadth of interest of Pasternak, who in 1927 celebrated his sixty-fifth birthday with a one-man exhibition at the Galerie Hartberg, in Berlin.

The success of the exhibition, both in terms of sales and press response, exceeded anything he had expected. Several dozen German and Russian newspaper clippings, still preserved, reveal widespread praise of the portraits, landscapes and still life studies, of the artist's unique qualities in use of line and colour.

Max Osborn, who was to write elsewhere at length about Pasternak, pointed

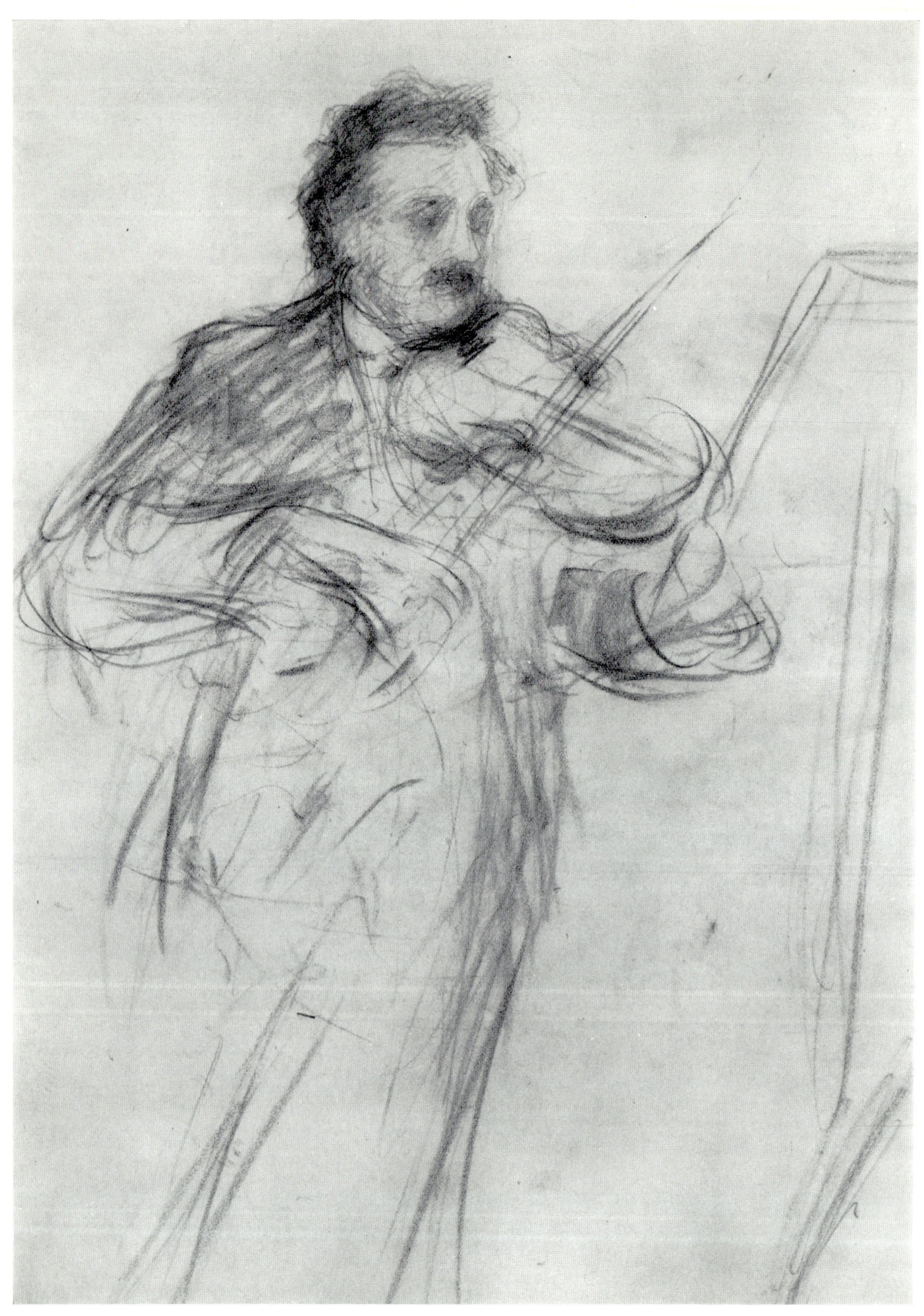

Einstein Playing the Violin, early 1920's, pencil, 35 × 25 cm.

out how he was nearly 60 when he moved to Germany in 1921. Yet he had quickly settled into the local artistic scene, and thereafter his work had gone on developing. 'A sound, uninhibited and genuine painter's temperament is at work here,' Osborn comments on the exhibition, 'a man who seizes his brush, mixes his colours and tackles the canvas with innate joy. Such a gift must find its fulfilment in Impressionism, which in Russia meant working in broad, vigorous brush-strokes. Only Pasternak added, born out of the Russian tradition which was closely connected with folk art, a stronger feeling for brilliant local colour. Especially in the last – the Berlin – years, this sensuous language of gay colours, which is the outcome of the fusion of the two influences, has begun to unfold splendidly. There are pictures of flowers which glow warmly. There are portraits of staggering virtuosity. Pasternak's people all live, natural and full of movement.'[47]

The portraits made a marked impression on the German critics, notably that of Lovis Corinth, Pasternak's fellow-student at Munich. Their friendship had been renewed when Pasternak visited Germany in 1906, and at least one writer in 1927 remarked on points of contact in the works of these two Impressionists of such dissimilar backgrounds. That most fastidious of critics, Fritz Stahl, is completely won over by 'a portrait of the master Lovis Corinth which is one of the very best portraits of contemporaries which I have ever seen'. He sketches in for the reader pertinent facts about Corinth who, although partly paralysed, had continued to produce fine paintings. 'Nobody would have believed that *this* Corinth of the last years was portrayable. Here he stands before us. It is an act of deeply understanding love and veneration which would regard it as a sacrilege to omit, to add or even to emphasize anything. Even the size and the medium (watercolour) are modest, and this very restraint in the external intensifies the spiritual content. This portrait should hang next to Corinth's latest work, which it would explain better than words. It proves Pasternak to be one of those born portraitists who are so very rare.'[48]

An interesting Russian view of Pasternak's exhibition was V. Tatarinov's, in the newspaper *Rul*, published in Berlin. Tatarinov was especially pleased that 'even such a strict critic as Stahl [has] fully appreciated the brilliance of the youthful brush of our non-ageing master' Pasternak. Tatarinov accepted that it was the general view 'that Russian art as compared to West European art has a relative value only; that it lacks independence; that it does not open up new vistas and repeats "other people's songs" '. This was the view not only of foreign but of some Russian critics, too, but he liked the Pasternak exhibition because it was not necessary to untangle metaphysical problems to appreciate the pictures. This was 'exceptional, for we are not used any more to seeing bright and fresh colours, sureness and precision of form and line, masterful composition, live flowers, live faces – really, in front of Pasternak's paintings and drawings you begin to doubt the truth of the above-mentioned opinions concerning Russian art'.[49]

Fritz Stahl, like several other German critics, emphasized the sound draughtsmanship underlying Pasternak's work, drawing attention to his Munich training. Anton Mayer thought that Pasternak had achieved his success with the Corinth portrait 'through the spirit of the colour; it is with this in mind that all Pasternak's work has to be seen. Colour, thank God, is his most personal artistic language; he interweaves it in thousands of delicate shades, he unfolds it over brilliant, luminous areas and while doing so always hits the *essence* of the matter, so that his pictures, although characterised by the painter's determined grasp, are never encumbered by the materialism of imitative painting'. Mayer found the same satisfying colour harmonies in the landscapes and flower still-lifes: 'the gladiolas and roses are just as alive as the human models, as is the sunlight on houses or gardens. In fact, it is very difficult to talk about details, for the work is characterized by a natural and self-evident formal unity, which makes us perceive it as a whole just as much as we are aware of its parts . . . .

'A series apart is made up of studies from Palestine,' notes Mayer. 'The Orient was bound to captivate as ardent a worshipper of colour as Pasternak . . . . In the pastels we admire the marvellously light, yet completely assured handling of the delicate medium'.[50] The trip to Egypt and Palestine had been a strange, exotic undertaking for Pasternak, which occurred in 1924. The publisher A. Kogan, whom Pasternak was later to paint, planned an exhaustive volume to be entitled *The Golden Book of Palestine,* which would cover the Holy Land from many aspects: geographically, ethnographically, culturally, historically, and so on. He invited Pasternak and several other artists to take part in an expedition to the area, so that the book could be lavishly illustrated. Pasternak at first refused this well-paid assignment. He was too old, he said, and his health was not good enough. The hardships and disturbances of the previous decade made him reluctant to leave his family circle, and he feared that they had blunted his sensibility to new experiences, that he would be artistically impotent.

By the time the expedition had reached Palestine, his friends in Germany had persuaded him to join it. The trip along the Greek coast and the arrival in Egypt were a revelation. In Egypt, that country 'only by a small strip of water separated from another, completely different world', he exhausted himself visiting the museums and art treasures.

Pasternak brought back numerous studies of Palestine. Here, suddenly, he was reminded of the achievement of the landscape painter Vassily Polenov, now an old man, whom he had met 35 years before and who had been such an influence on him. It had been in the 1880's that Polenov had completed his scenes from the life of Christ. 'I left the car and turned round: the Genissaret lake stretched in front of me in all its majestic grandeur,' Pasternak writes. 'To the left Tiberias exhaling the palpitating white heat of its mosques and little houses softly drew the curve of the coastal surf; in the opposite direction the violet-rosy background stretched, with the scarcely visible top of the Hermon. And such quiet around,

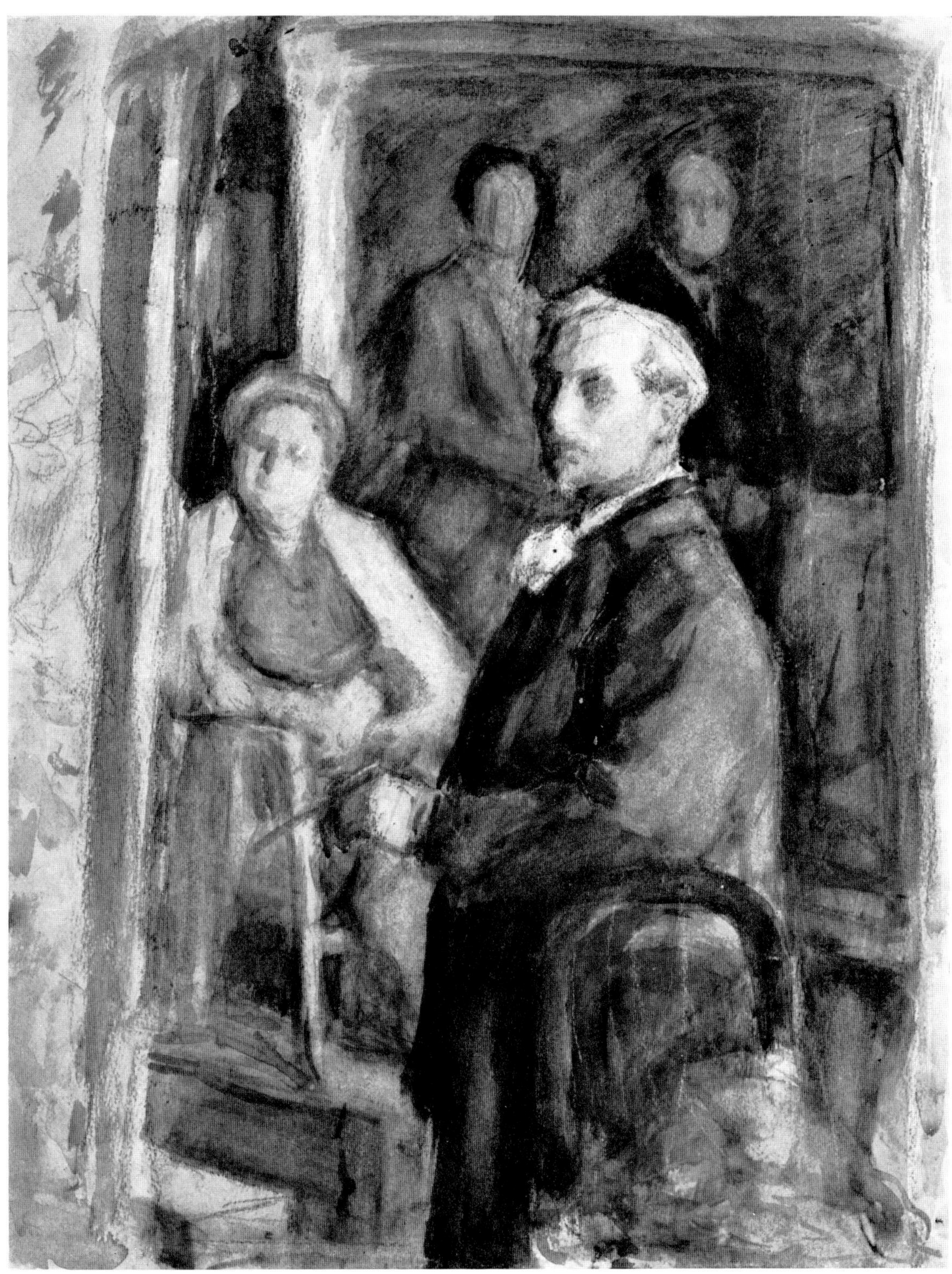

The Artist and his Wife in Front of a Portrait, 1920's, watercolour, 34 × 26·5 cm.

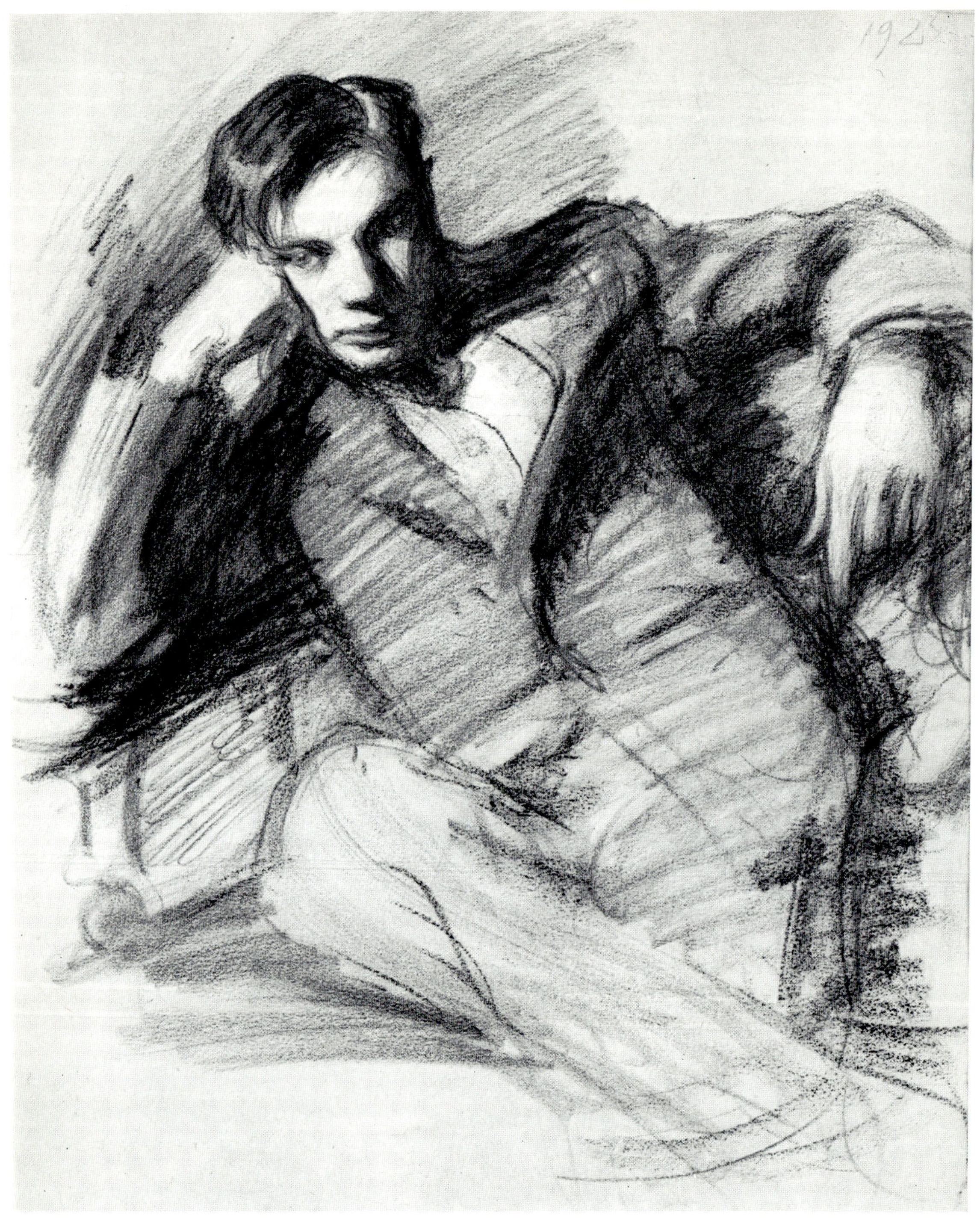

Portrait of the Artist's Son Alexander, 1925, charcoal, 38 × 30·5 cm.

such inexpressible sublime calm . . . . "My God!" I exclaimed, "but all this is Polenov!" Polenov's was that dark blue-violet Mediterranean sea foaming at the sides of the ship, with those sunset-pink mountains of the Greek isles . . . Polenov's all the astounding scenery on the way to Tiberias – all this harmony of colours which had moved me so much – all around was Polenov's palette! Here only, in the very places committed to memory by his brush, can one understand and assess adequately his enormous colouristic gift, here only can one measure the depth of his penetration into the landscape of Palestine.'

Back in Germany Pasternak continued to work hard, the pictures in the 1927 exhibition being the result. The success of that show spurred him on further. Inspiration for portraits and landscapes came also from the annual summer holiday journey that he and Rosa made to southern Bavaria and Munich, where their elder daughter Josephine now lived. Many fine studies of the Bavarian mountains and lakes originated from these vacations. A typical picture from the period is an impressive oil of Schliersee, the lake and surrounding trees, with Rosa and Josephine Pasternak sitting on a balcony, now in the family collection at Oxford. The scene is a medley of powdery pinks, blues and greens that are so typical of Pasternak's oils. Although completed several decades later, its colouring is reminiscent of the early *genre* canvas *A Letter from Home*, indicating the continuity in his work despite all intervening events.

Occasionally Rosa would play the piano for friends, although it was years since she had appeared on a public platform. The doubt which Leonid had felt about marrying her and robbing her of a musical career in the late 1880's apparently still smouldered fitfully. Josephine Pasternak recalls one incident which took place during a Bavarian holiday, when the family was staying with friends. 'In the evenings we had music. One day mother was asked to take part in it too . . . . She chose Beethoven's sonatas, the very late ones, least known to the public. When she had finished there was a general hush. With mother's modest bearing, no one had expected her to give such a masterly interpretation. When later in the evening we were back in our rooms upstairs, in a voice of pure admiration father said: "I now realise that I ought not to have married you. It was my fault. You have sacrificed your genius to me and the family. Of us two you are the greater artist." '[51]

The success of his second one-man show, again at the Galerie Hartberg, Berlin, in 1932 was, however, a reminder of Leonid Pasternak's considerable achievement. He had no doubt that in the five years since 1927 and the first show his technique had developed. He had many new pictures to display. In addition, to celebrate his seventieth birthday a lavishly illustrated monograph was produced, which included a critical text by Max Osborn. With its extensive reproductions, many in colour, the volume is now a collector's item.* Pasternak closely super-

---

Leonid Pasternak. By Max Osborn, Stybel (Warsaw 1932), in German.

vised the reproductions, calling at the printer's to discuss work in hand, so that some drawings as printed are indistinguishable from the originals. The artist also contributed four fragments of autobiography – childhood reminiscences and encounters with Tolstoy, Rilke and Lovis Corinth. 'This richly produced book . . . brings before our eyes a considerable stretch of world history,' writes the critic of *Vossische Zeitung*, 'from pre-war Russia up to the revolutionary Soviet regime, from Tolstoy, Gordon Craig, Nikisch, Hermann Cohen to von Harnack, Corinth, Chaliapin, Liebermann, Einstein, Hauptmann, Lenin. Thus Pasternak's work surpasses its aesthetic significance to assume historical importance.'[52]

The second Hartberg exhibition, taking place as it did close to the painter's seventieth birthday, prompted many critics to review Pasternak's overall achievement and to examine the roots of his inspiration. B. E. Werner remarked that the works of his Berlin period 'mark the journey of Impressionism from West to East. The quick, sketchy impressionist recording of optical experiences is just as characteristic of the artist as the expansive Russian love of colour. The old gentleman is inspired by a fine temperament, by the untiring clinging to the gods of youth, which is hardly diverted by the clearly observable encounter with Corinth'.[53] Curt Glaser believed that the older Russian school, of which Pasternak was 'one of the most capable painters', had formulated an art which 'is mistakenly called Impressionism. It would, of course, have been impossible without Manet and Monet. But their style is generally European, and it distinguishes itself from the latter only by some national Russian features which are difficult to define'.[54]

For some critics an examination of Pasternak's antecedents was unimportant when they came face-to-canvas with a gallery full of such landscapes, still-lifes and portraits, which again excited much comment. Thus the *Steglitzer Anzeiger's* critic thought that: 'To describe this art – a sensuous abandonment to the outward visual world – as belonging to a long-lost, unproblematic past, and to call it Impressionism, does not exhaust the essence of these cultivated pictures. The wonderful, and very personal, thing about these exuberant still-lifes of flowers and distinguished portraits is the optimistic affirmation of life which they exude.'[55] The critic of *Volkszeitung*, Berlin, was in no doubt that Pasternak was 'a great master of the Impressionist School, a wonderful portrayer of human beings. Everything is painted in soft, warm colours – it is the Russian soul which we seem to be able to feel through these pictures. The portraits of Gerhardt Hauptmann, Rainer Maria Rilke and well-known musicians are some of the most noble and excellent achievements in the portraiture of our time'.[56]

Perhaps the most perceptive article to stem from the 1932 exhibition, certainly one of the best pieces ever written on the artist in his lifetime, was the long, well-illustrated one by Carl Meissner in the magazine *Westermanns Monatshefte* towards the end of the year, when the publicity furore had abated. Meissner relates Pasternak to the entire development of Russian art up to his time, and in doing so makes some good points. He had interviewed Pasternak at length, 'this artist who, when one says to him after a long and vivid conversation: "Professor, do take a seat!" answers: "Oh no – I am on my feet the whole day, anyway." '[57]

Meissner maintains that the Russian temperament had caused men like Pasternak to excel in painting rather than in, say, architecture or sculpture, as 'often a painting is the result of an intense and concentrated effort – lasting, however, only a few hours'. Pasternak was typical of the modern painters of his country because 'man is more important to the Russian than landscape. They were too emotional and restless to be able to meditate quietly or to sink into contemplation, and were consequently particularly susceptible to the deeply stirring influence of Impressionism, and the light palette'. Where Pasternak was untypical was in his not being completely Russian, coming from the southern port of Odessa, where the population had constantly mingled with Italian and Spanish blood.

Meissner considers that 'it is a general truth that precisely those artists with the most profound understanding of the character of their people are often not of the same blood. It liberates their way of looking at things and they can therefore see from above and from the outside what at the same time they know and feel instinctively already . . . . Pasternak's knowledge of the Russian world is so profound, his compositions so well-balanced and assured, his use of painting techniques, especially of light, so discriminating, that his hands, similar to those of a pianist that assuredly hit the keys, succeed in recreating in a masterly way the infinite variations of the Russian atmosphere . . . . Leonid Pasternak is an Impressionist – particularly strongly so in his drawings, even despite their forcefulness – but as he does not let the light let his colour go grey or lose its brilliance when painting in oils, Pasternak is also a colourist, a powerful colourist even'.

Although now in his seventies, Pasternak continued to work. The small drawing-pad and pencil that always accompanied him remained at hand to record fleeting impressions, sometimes as reminders for a future picture. Now the rise to power of Hitler, a desire to see his sons again and to teach the younger generation of Russian painters prompted thoughts of a return to Moscow. There Alexander was practising as an architect and Boris had established his reputation as a poet.

They were in regular contact by telephone and letter. In a letter written in 1934 Boris comments: 'I am now as old as you were in 1906 in Berlin. It is enough for me to remember you at that period to shrink back from the comparison. You were a real man . . . a Colossus, and before this image, large and wide as the world, I am a complete nonentity and in every respect still a boy . . . . I have been looking through your monograph again, after a long period of time, and was suddenly struck by the impact of your personality. What a wonderful artist you are! . . . In your place, with such a life behind you, I should feel in the seventh heaven. Such a life, such a hand, such encounters and recollections!'[58]

The Pasternaks now planned seriously their return to Russia, discussing it with the Soviet ambassador and other officials in Berlin. Soon a flat for them was being sought in Moscow, and there were tentative plans for an exhibition of Leonid's work there. The worry of sorting and packing the accumulated belongings of years, however, proved a strain on them both. Leonid, who had had delicate health in his youth but since had never suffered a serious illness, was now to experience the first symptoms of angina.

The old freedom of Berlin which they had enjoyed from the 1920's had given way to the unbearable atmosphere of Nazi Germany. Moreover, Soviet citizens were gradually being arrested or expelled. The Pasternaks accepted an invitation from their younger daughter, Lydia, who had married an Englishman, to visit them in London, to rest and recuperate before going back to Russia. But it was another two or three years before they finally left Germany, soon followed by Josephine, her husband and their two children. 'Sick, tired and incapable of any new undertaking,' as Pasternak puts it, they made their second journey to England in the spring of 1938. They still planned a return to Moscow, but England was to prove their final move.

Last Years in England
Pasternak's daughter Josephine says that her father, who like many artists had suffered material hardship when young, was a man who did not readily complain when the going was tough. He held that suffering was an inevitable part of life, even a refiner of character. This stoicism was to be put to the test during the early days of his second visit to England. Berlin, celebrity and well-being was exchanged for South London, drab anonymity and a long succession of debilitating illnesses.

This gloomy period of Pasternak's life was lightened by work, by the presence of the children and grandchildren and by a handful of old friends from Russia and Germany. Among their new friends was Arthur M. Hind, artist and director of the Print Room at the British Museum, whose pencil portrait Pasternak completed around this time. Like the other members of his family he was a keen musician, and it was at his house that Rosa was invited to play the piano part in her favourite Schumann quintet in the summer of 1939. Although aged 72, musically she was still active, but this was the last time she played for an audience. As in the past there were calls for encores – Bach and Chopin. Two months later, during a terrible thunderstorm, she had a stroke, and died three days after it.

The effect on Pasternak was devastating. There had been talk of an exhibition in London, about which Rosa had been especially enthusiastic. Then there had been the plan to return to Moscow, worked out in Berlin and discussed with the Soviet Embassy in London. In fact, on the day of his wife's stroke, Leonid was due to see Maisky, the Soviet ambassador, for the final arrangements. Nothing seemed of any importance now. Then came the Stalin-Hitler pact, and shortly afterwards war was declared. It seemed a mercy that Rosa had been spared all this, yet Pasternak continued to hope to see Russia again.

In poor health he moved with his daughters and their families to Oxford. It was in the home of his younger daughter that he began to pick up his life again. He found Oxford quaint and described the English as an aristocratic people. He especially liked to visit the Ashmolean Museum, which now has a substantial collection of his work. And he began to work once more. A drawing of Gilbert Slater, principal of Ruskin College, shows no decline in his draughtsman's powers. There were oil portraits, too, and a large number of historical compositions, such as *Bach and Frederick the Great, The Young Mendelssohn Conducting Bach, Tolstoy at his Writing Desk, Scenes from Soviet Life* and *Pushkin with his Nurse*. Now that he was busy again Pasternak was approached about an English exhibition, but he decided that it would best be postponed until after the war.

Josephine Pasternak gives us some fascinating glimpses of her father's life during those early war years in Oxford. It was natural that his thoughts often turned to happier times in Russia and Germany, and his daughters sensibly took advantage of this looking back. 'We pressed father to write his reminiscences. Some evenings when the light was too poor for his artistic work, he would sit down at his table, and page after page, memories of bygone days would be resuscitated in a lively narration. Or he would just jot down a few notes.'[59] Pasternak did not speak much English, and it was in the books in which he did his language exercises that many of his recollections were written. 'We were busy with our small children, and whenever we had a chance to be together, we found ourselves merely chatting with each other. Only many years after father's death did I come across his notes. His writings reflect not only a whole period of Russian life and culture, but also the painter's own moods and beliefs, his views on art, and his judgements in matters of topical interest.'

Recollecting the events of the previous 80 years revived memories of people and places that had sometimes lain dormant a long time. These would provide subjects for conversation with his daughters, and with pleasure Pasternak would recall visits to the frescoes of Campo Santo, in Pisa, the art of the Quattrocento in Florence and Tuscany, seeing Giorgione's, Titian's and Tintoretto's canvases in Venice and other masterpieces in northern European galleries. The catholicity of his taste was shown by his high regard for early Chinese painting and for the Egyptian portraitists, whose works he had seen in the 1920's. 'Thousands of years separate us,' he would say, 'yet I can feel the bodily presence of the artist, as if he was standing next to me, a brother of mine, and as if I could reach out and press his hand.'

'Father thought of draughtsmanship as the cornerstone of all arts,' writes Josephine Pasternak, 'and quoted Michelangelo and Ingres accordingly. He regarded the latter and Delacroix as the progenitors of modern European art. He was fascinated by Turner whom he considered as being the first Impressionist, he admired Manet, Degas, and Renoir, he gave Gauguin his due, and he acknowledged Picasso as an accomplished draughtsman. Of his Russian fellow-artists he revered the icon-painters, A. Ivanov, Polenov, and Repin. Of the artists of his own age group Serov was the nearest to him.'

There were frequent visitors to the house in Park Town where Pasternak lived, which provided him with constant interest. His daughter Lydia made it a type of sanctuary for European refugees, London evacuees and other people without a home. 'With bewilderment, yet sometimes with a twinkle in his eye, father used to look at this motley crowd, who sometimes behaved very oddly indeed,' his elder daughter recalls. Occasionally there would be a visit from a journalist, for although Pasternak's arrival in England a few years before had passed unnoticed, in 1942, when he celebrated his eightieth birthday, it was covered in the local and national press.

An exhibition was still in Pasternak's mind. There was talk of one in Oxford, and in 1942 Pasternak received a visit from I. M. Maisky, the Soviet ambassador. The artist agreed to lend some pictures for a show of Russian pictures to be held in England to aid the Soviet Red Cross and Red Crescent organizations. The suggestion was that one room should be given over to Pasternak's works, but the scheme fell through when the right premises could not be found.[60]

Pasternak, the born pacifist and Tolstoy's friend, was often in pensive mood as the war spread. His notes made during this time show how pessimistic he was about the future. 'The scarcity of news from his sons and relations in Russia distressed him profoundly,' writes his daughter Josephine.[61] 'Used to his sense of reality, his religious firmness, and his somewhat ironic attitude towards philosophising, it was with a stab of pain that one day I heard him say: "What *is* the meaning of life?" He must have looked into an abyss of suffering if he could have asked this question with such pathetic submissiveness.' Usually he was noted for his optimism and sense of proportion, even during the war's darkest days. 'Chance visitors and strangers who happened to call at Park Town would be reassured, and regained hope after a talk with him. He admired Churchill: "Oh, how wise this man is. Don't you worry: he will see his country through to final victory." '

Pasternak was painting to the end, a portrait of Lenin being the last picture on his easel. He died in Oxford on 31 May 1945, aged 83.

Posthumous Exhibitions

Obituaries of Leonid Pasternak were published widely in England and abroad, although wartime newsprint shortage clearly reduced their size. In 1945 there was again talk of an exhibition, but one was not arranged until 1958. Apart from the several major shows that have taken place in England and Germany there have been a number of private or semi-public ones. Inevitably, too, with an artist who spent his life depicting men as famous as Tolstoy, Lenin and Einstein, Pasternak's works are often required to strengthen exhibitions associated with such figures.

One of the smaller shows took place in Moscow in May 1969, comprising pictures drawn from private collections. It is of special interest because of the opening address by Evgeny Levitin, head of the Department of Graphic Arts in the Pushkin Museum of Fine Arts, Moscow – a rare informed contemporary assessment of Pasternak in his own country. Levitin saw Pasternak as a key figure in the transition to modern art in Russia. 'Pasternak was one of the first to break with academism, and to introduce light, air and colour into his work. He is the greatest representative of Russian Impressionism . . . . His role in the fields of drawing and illustration is to be particularly noted. More than any other artist, Pasternak stressed the importance of good draughtsmanship, and the combination of spontaneity and liveliness with firm structure was the new and outstanding characteristic of his drawings . . . .

'As for illustration, Pasternak's drawings for Tolstoy's *Resurrection*, and his work in bringing into being and editing the large illustrated edition of Lermontov's works marked, in fact, the very birth of Russian illustrative art. This was true illustration of the text, not the provision of mere types or pictures on a theme! . . . The bulk of our postwar illustrations, until the most recent times, represent a development of Pasternak's traditions . . . . In the large extant mass of Tolstoyana his work undoubtedly holds the first place. It is perhaps worth remembering here that Tolstoy's last secretary, the late Valentin Bulgakov, emphatically maintained that Pasternak's portraits of Tolstoy are the most lifelike.'[62]

The major one-man exhibitions since Pasternak's death owe much to the effort and enthusiasm of his daughters, Josephine and Lydia, who still live in Oxford. It was there in 1958 that the Ashmolean Museum put on a memorial show, the first in England. This was so successful that it had to be extended from April into May. Sir Maurice Bowra in the catalogue drew attention to Pasternak's gift for portrait drawing. 'He felt that if his first sketch did not catch the essential character of his subject, he had failed and must start again . . . . Pasternak's picture of intellectual and artistic Russia, before and during the Revolution, is indeed a historical record of the highest richness and worth. But it is more than this. For it is a record which only an artist could have produced, who saw these men in their rich and varied individuality and caught them in their unguarded, unconscious poses and their characteristic gestures and expressions . . . . In all his portraits there is the same unerring sense of personality, the gift for presenting a man not through his superficial traits but through his real character.'[63]

A further exhibition was held in 1958 at the Pushkin Club, London, in October-November. The theme of the show, which gained substantial press coverage, was 'The Russian Scene'. Frederick Laws, while pointing out that the exhibition 'deserves to be visited for its historical or documentary interest even apart from its artistic merit', made the good point that, as with many skilled portrait painters, much of Pasternak's best work was not of famous public figures, but was domestic. 'To draw conclusions about life in Russia at any given date would not be easy except domestically. The artist loved painting his own family or the families of his friends at meals, at music, teaching or playing with the children, or reading in the lamplight. It is a warm, kind, closed-in world not unlike that which delighted Bonnard.'[64]

The centenary year of Pasternak's birth, 1962, saw three exhibitions – Städtische Galerie, Munich, in August, Herbert Art Gallery and Museum, Coventry, in September–October and Bristol Museum and Art Gallery, in December 1962–January 1963. The substantial press coverage of the Munich exhibition indicated the regard that Germany still has for his work. Writers were aware of the bond between Pasternak and German Impressionism.

The critic of *Stuttgarter Zeitung* perceived similarities between the Russian artist and Adolf Menzel. 'Like Menzel he was indefatigable with his pencil . . . . A delicate gradation of chiaroscuro envelops the forms, the figures, which have the softness of anonymity. The light and dark masses are distributed throughout the picture with generous strokes, but every now and then, at a detail such as a hand or the hair caught by the light, the pencil lingers in a lovingly curling movement. One thinks of Degas, more even of Renoir. In Pasternak's pastels there is the same generous distribution of colour-masses dominated by the rhythm of the chiaroscuro, the tones are warm, the shades soft'.[65]

How well Pasternak exploits the domestic scene was perceived by several critics in Munich. In his opening address, too, the gallery's director, Dr. Röthel, had drawn attention to Pasternak's dictum: 'The nursery is the best academy'. The critic of *Schwarzwalder Zeitung 'Der Grenzer'* was interested in how time and again Pasternak 'had drawn and painted his wife and children, now on the morning of a birthday, admiring the flowers, now reading or writing, now playing the piano, now engaged in the colouring of Easter-eggs. In his drawings, with a convincing stroke, he arrests momentary movements and positions'.[66] Another critic noted that 'The limited number of exhibits and the modest dimensions of the exhibition rooms were in harmony with the intimate, exceptionally fascinating character of Pasternak's work. One would like to own nearly all these pictures – how seldom can one say that'.[67]

One topic that took the attention of *AZ-Feuilleton*'s critic was the double portrait which had caused such a sensation in the 1920's and 1930's, 'Lovis Corinth painted by Pasternak and Leonid Pasternak painted by Corinth. While the Pasternak portrait was shown some years ago at the major Corinth exhibition in Munich, the companion picture seems to have been lost in the confusion of the Third Reich. When Josephine Pasternak talks about this picture one feels, however, that secretly she still hopes for a great surprise: that this portrait of Corinth will turn up some day'.[68]

Pasternak's drawing was the feature of his work commented on by critics attending the two 1962 English exhibitions. Luke Herrmann, whilst acknowledging that Pasternak was 'strongly influenced by the work of the Impressionists', felt that he was 'essentially a Russian artist. His strivings for purity of form, and for vitality in his renderings of light and colour, always retained something of the firm and positive approach associated with the traditional Russian art of the icon', for 'the basis of all his work was his confident draughtsmanship'. Herrmann repeated the story that Pasternak tells in one of his fragments of autobiography, how a drawing he had made when a schoolboy of some Siamese twins had so moved his usually harsh headmaster that he had led Leonid by the hand into his flat to show the drawing to his wife.[69]

Douglas Wollen, who was able to see more of the artist's pictures privately in Oxford, singled out 'what must surely be Pasternak's masterpiece' *The Silver Wedding Morning*, which dates from 1914 and shows the children bearing gifts for their parents. 'The whole display is a hymn of praise of family life, and, to use a phrase which should surely be applicable to any aesthetic delight, it does the viewer good.'[70]

In March–May 1969 the Oxford University Press organised a Pasternak exhibition at Ely House, Dover Street, in London. Among appreciations of it, the one by Terence Mullaly was perhaps the most perceptive, concentrating on the artist as portrait painter. He found Pasternak 'a kind of Russian Vuillard, recording the intimate scene with gentle humanity. Yet this was not all. He was also a draughtsman of decision; not many artists of our time have combined such good drawing with as much sympathy and understanding . . . . Few roles are more exacting than that of the portrait painter . . . . It requires a rare amalgam of detachment, shrewd observation, and care for the human situation. Leonid Pasternak was endowed with all these qualities'.[71]

References

[1] *The Times*, 2 January 1957.
[2] The Pasternak quotations throughout are from extensive notes discovered in Oxford after he died there, in 1945. These are to be published in Russian in the Soviet Union with a linking commentary by his daughter Josephine, who has worked on them for some years.
[3] BORIS PASTERNAK. *Fifty Poems*. Translated and with an introduction by Lydia Pasternak-Slater. George Allen and Unwin Ltd (London 1963) page 18.
[4] *Ibid.*, page 21.
[5] Quoted *ibid.*, page 18.
[6] Quoted in KAYE WEBB. Tolstoy's Artist in Oxford. *Lilliput* (January 1944) pages 63–6.
[7] CARL MEISSNER. Leonid Pasternak. *Westermanns Monatshefte* (November 1932) pages 213–20.
[8] LEONID PASTERNAK. My Meetings with Tolstoy. *The Mediterranean Review* (Volume 2 Number 1 1970) pages 8–11.
[9] N. MOLEVA and E. BELIUTIN. *Russian Art Schools of the Second Half of the XIX and Beginning of the XX Century*. Art (Moscow 1967) page 256, in Russian.
[10] BORIS PASTERNAK. *An Essay in Autobiography*. Translated by Manya Harari, with an introduction by Edward Crankshaw. Collins and Harvill Press (London 1959) page 30.
[11] My Meetings with Tolstoy, *op. cit.*
[12] *An Essay in Autobiography, op. cit.*, pages 37–8.
[13] My Meetings with Tolstoy, *op. cit.*
[14] *An Essay in Autobiography, op. cit.*, pages 39–40.
[15] *Ibid.*, pages 29–30.
[16] *Ibid.*, pages 32–3.
[17] *Fifty Poems, op. cit.*, page 19.
[18] Tolstoy's Artist in Oxford, *op. cit.*
[19] My Meetings with Tolstoy, *op. cit.*
[20] *An Essay in Autobiography, op. cit.*, pages 34–5.
[21] BORIS PASTERNAK. *Safe Conduct* – an Early Autobiography and other Works. Translated by Alec Brown, Five Lyric Poems translated by Lydia Pasternak-Slater. Elek Books (London 1959) page 188.
[22] Quoted in *Fifty Poems, op. cit.*, page 16.
[23] ALEXANDER PASTERNAK. Skryabin: Summer 1903 and after. Translated by Felicity Ashbee and Irina Tidmarsh from an article in *Novy Mir*. *Musical Times* (December 1972) page 1,171.
[24] Vacksel Archive 3269, Department of Manuscripts at the Saltykov-Shchedrin State Public Library, in Russian.
[25] Quoted in CAMILLA GRAY. *The Russian Experiment in Art 1863–1922*. Thames and Hudson (London 1971) pages 9–10.
[26] *Ibid.*, page 15.
[27] *Ibid.*, page 39.
[28] *Ibid.*, page 44.
[29] ALEXANDRE BENOIS. *Memoirs.* Translated by Moura Budberg. Chatto and Windus (London 1964) volume 2, page 166.
[30] V. D. POLENOV and E. D. POLENOVA. *The Artists' Family Chronicle*. E. V. Sakharova. Art (Moscow 1964) pages 455–6, in Russian.
[31] *Ibid.*, page 554.
[32] *Ibid.*, pages 554–5.
[33] Y. D. MINTCHENKOV. *Reminiscences of the Wanderers*. The Artist in R.S.F.S.R. (Leningrad 1963) page 327.
[34] I. E. REPIN. *Birjeviye Vedomosti*, 15 May 1910.
[35] PRINCE SERGE SCHERBATOFF. *The Artist in Old Russia*. Chekhov Publishing House (U.S.A. 1955) page 123.
[36] *Ibid.*, pages 115, 123.
[37] *An Essay in Autobiography, op. cit.*, pages 52–3.
[38] *Ibid.*, page 61.
[39] *Ibid.*, pages 59–60.
[40] P. ETTINGER. The Drawings of L. Pasternak. *The Studio* (15 May 1906) pages 306–13.
[41] NIKOLAUS PEVSNER, IAN NAIRN and BRIDGET CHERRY. *The Buildings of England: Surrey*. Penguin Books (Harmondsworth 1971) page 223.
[42] *An Essay in Autobiography, op. cit.*, page 63.
[43] *Ibid.*, page 89.
[44] *Ibid.*, page 72.
[45] S. BURDIANSKY. Dear Features. *Isvestia*, Moscow evening issue, 5 November 1965.
[46] *Letters of Rainer Maria Rilke, 1892–1926.* Translated by Jane Bannard Greene and M. D. Herter Norton. W. W. Norton and Co. Inc. (New York 1948) volume 2, page 386.
[47] MAX OSBORN. Leonid Pasternak, Exhibition at Hartberg's. *Vossische Zeitung*, 24 December 1927.
[48] FRITZ STAHL. Exhibitions. *Berliner Tageblatt*, 21 December 1927.
[49] V. TATARINOV. *Rul*, 30 December 1927, in Russian.
[50] ANTON MAYER. Leonid Pasternak, Exhibition at Hartberg's. *8-Uhr-Abendblatt*, 17 December 1927.
[51] JOSEPHINE PASTERNAK. Foreword to exhibition catalogue of Pasternak's Works, Oxford University Press, Ely House, London, March–May 1969.
[52] MAX OSBORN. Leonid Pasternak. *Vossische Zeitung*, 29 May 1932.
[53] B. E. WERNER. *Deutsche Allgemeine Zeitung*, 12 March 1932.

[54] CURT GLASER. Notes on Exhibitions. *Berliner Börsen-Courier*, 9 March 1932.

[55] Art Chronicle. *Steglitzer Anzeiger*, 30 March 1932.

[56] Contrasts in Art – Exhibitions of Beckmann and Pasternak. *Volkszeitung*, Berlin, 10 March 1932.

[57] Leonid Pasternak. *Westermanns Monatshefte*, *op. cit.*, page 213.

[58] Quoted in *Fifty Poems*, *op. cit.*, pages 15–16.

[59] Oxford University Press catalogue foreword, *op. cit.*

[60] S. BURDIANSKY. A New Encounter with Il'itch. *The Week* (28 November–4 December 1965), in Russian.

[61] Oxford University Press exhibition catalogue foreword, *op. cit.*

[62] EVGENY LEVITIN. Opening speech at exhibition of Pasternak's works, Club of Private Collectors, at the House of the Printer, Moscow, May 1969, in Russian.

[63] C. M. BOWRA. Foreword to exhibition catalogue of Pasternak's works, Ashmolean Museum, Oxford, April–May 1958.

[64] FREDERICK LAWS. Paintings, drawings and watercolours of Pasternak. *The Manchester Guardian*, 10 October 1958.

[65] Pasternak Senior, *Stuttgarter Zeitung*, 10 August 1962.

[66] Drawings by Leonid Pasternak. *Schwarzwalder Zeitung 'Der Grenzer'*, 11 August 1962.

[67] From Munich Galleries. *Die Weltkunst* (September 1962).

[68] In Memory of the Russian Painter Leonid Pasternak. *AZ-Feuilleton*, 3 August 1962.

[69] LUKE HERRMANN. Portraits by a Pasternak. *The Sunday Telegraph*, 8 April 1962.

[70] DOUGLAS WOLLEN. Pasternak's Pictures. *The Times*, 19 April 1962.

[71] TERENCE MULLALY. Pasternak the Elder. *The Daily Telegraph*, 24 May 1969.

J. B. Manson, an English Impressionist
By David Buckman

This is the first published account of Manson's career, as painter, writer and director of the Tate Gallery, from 1930–38. It draws on previously largely unpublished correspondence between him and Lucien Pissarro, held in the Ashmolean Museum. Manson was a founder-member of the Camden Town and London Groups, and the monograph gives a short account of the Monarro Group, inspired by Monet and Camille Pissarro, which Manson and Lucien founded just after the First World War. Bound in soft covers, $9\frac{5}{8} \times 7$ in., 56 pages, 25 plates (one in colour). Price £1·80

'Manson was esteemed for his fine impressionist paintings. This new study reveals that he was also a fascinating and kindly man' – Brian Wallworth, *Arts Review*

'A compactly informative memoir' – William Gaunt, *The Times*

'An admirable book' – Marina Vaizey, *The Financial Times*

Published by the Maltzahn Gallery Ltd

(Distributed to the trade by Cranfield and Bonfiel Books)

Robert Bevan
A catalogue raisonné of the lithographs and other prints

Increasing interest in the Camden Town Group makes this catalogue of prints by the artist Robert Bevan a welcome addition to our knowledge of his art. Graham Dry has recorded, annotated and illustrated all 40 Bevan prints – three etchings, 36 lithographs and one wood engraving. There is an informative note by the artist's son, R. A. Bevan. Bound in buckram, crown quarto, 48 pages, 40 plates. Price £1·80

Published by the Maltzahn Gallery Ltd

(Distributed to the trade by Cranfield and Bonfiel Books)

Arthur Boyd
Etchings and lithographs

Arthur Boyd, born in Melbourne in 1920, has achieved a reputation as an artist far outside his native Australia. He came to London in 1959, having his first London exhibition, at the Zwemmer Gallery, in 1960. In 1962 he embarked seriously on etching and lithography. This book is devoted to the entire graphic work produced between 1962–9, with the exception of the St. Francis lithographs. There is an introduction by Imre von Maltzahn. Cloth bound, $9\frac{1}{2} \times 9\frac{1}{2}$ in., 140 pages, 120 plates (six in colour). Price £5·25

Published by Lund Humphries/Maltzahn Gallery Ltd

(Distributed to the trade by Lund Humphries)